eBay's Secrets Revealed:

The Insider's Guide to Advertising, Marketing, and Promoting Your eBay Store

With Little or No Money

By Dan W. Blacharski

eBay's Secrets Revealed: The Insider's Guide to Advertising, Marketing, and Promoting Your eBay Store—With Little or No Money

ISBN-13: 978-0-910627-86-3 ISBN-10: 0-910627-86-X

Library of Congress Cataloging-in-Publication Data

Blacharski, Dan, 1959-
eBay's Secrets revealed: the insider's guide to advertising, marketing, and promoting your eBay store, with little or no money / Author: Dan Blacharski
    p. cm.
    Includes bibliographical references and index.
    ISBN-13: 978-0-910627-86-3 (alk. paper)
    ISBN-10: 0-910627-86-X (alk. paper)
    1. eBay (Firm) 2. Internet Auctions. I. Title.

    HF5478.B53.2007
    658.8'7--dc22
                    2007009076

EDITOR: Marie Lujanac • mlujanac817@yahoo.com
ART DIRECTION: Meg Buchner • megadesn@mchsi.com
INTERIOR DESIGN: Michelle Bennett • mbennettdesign@yahoo.com

Printed in the United States

Printed on Recycled Paper

We recently lost our beloved pet "Bear," who was not only
our best and dearest friend but also the "Vice President of
Sunshine" here at Atlantic Publishing. He did not receive
a salary but worked tirelessly 24 hours a day to please
his parents. Bear was a rescue dog that turned around
and showered myself, my wife Sherri, his grandparents
Jean, Bob and Nancy and every person and animal he met
(maybe not rabbits) with friendship and love. He made a
lot of people smile every day.

We wanted you to know that a portion of the profits of this
book will be donated to The Humane Society of
the United States.

–Douglas & Sherri Brown

THE HUMANE SOCIETY OF THE UNITED STATES©

The human-animal bond is as old as human history. We cherish our animal companions for their unconditional affection and acceptance. We feel a thrill when we glimpse wild creatures in their natural habitat or in our own backyard.

Unfortunately, the human-animal bond has at times been weakened. Humans have exploited some animal species to the point of extinction.

The Humane Society of the United States makes a difference in the lives of animals here at home and worldwide. The HSUS is dedicated to creating a world where our relationship with animals is guided by compassion. We seek a truly humane society in which animals are respected for their intrinsic value, and where the human-animal bond is strong.

Want to help animals? We have plenty of suggestions. Adopt a pet from a local shelter, join The Humane Society and be a part of our work to help companion animals and wildlife. You will be funding our educational, legislative, investigative and outreach projects in the U.S. and across the globe.

Or perhaps you'd like to make a memorial donation in honor of a pet, friend or relative? You can through our Kindred Spirits program. And if you'd like to contribute in a more structured way, our Planned Giving Office has suggestions about estate planning, annuities, and even gifts of stock that avoid capital gains taxes.

Maybe you have land that you would like to preserve as a lasting habitat for wildlife. Our Wildlife Land Trust can help you. Perhaps the land you want to share is a backyard—that's enough. Our Urban Wildlife Sanctuary Program will show you how to create a habitat for your wild neighbors.

So you see, it's easy to help animals. And The HSUS is here to help.

The Humane Society of the United States
2100 L Street NW
Washington, DC 20037
202-452-1100
www.hsus.org

CONTENTS

Chapter 4 Your E-mail Ad Campaign 45

Chapter 5 Inventory 55

Chapter 6 Payments 63

Chapter 7 Accounting and Taxes 71

Chapter 8 Preventing Fraud 79

Chapter 9 Security 89

Chapter 10 Get Positive Feedback 97

Chapter 11 Cross-Sell and Up-Sell 105

Chapter 12 Photography 115

Chapter 13 Writing Your eBay Text 123

Chapter 14 The Power of Text 133

Chapter 15 The eBay Listing 141

Chapter 16 Finding Products 149

Chapter 17 Pricing Strategies and Starting Bids 159

Chapter 18 Branching Out 167

Chapter 19 Creating a "Sticky" Site 175

Chapter 20 Search Engine Optimization and PPC Ads 183

Chapter 21 Optimizing eBay Search 191

Chapter 22 Customer Service 199

Chapter 23 A Growth Strategy 211

Chapter 24 Nickels and Dimes 221

Chapter 25 Selling Individual Items Versus Bulk 231

Chapter 26 Auctions Versus "Buy It Now," Fixed-Price Listings, and Other Alternatives 237

Chapter 27 How Do They Know You Are Legit? 245

Chapter 28 Auction Management Tools 251

Chapter 29 The Anonymous Seller 259

Chapter 30 eBay Tips For Success 265

About the Author 269

eBay Terminology 271

Index 279

Appendix 283

FOREWORD

By Kenneth L. Mills

Multiple eBay Power Seller Accounts
Primary Selling eBay blackknighttrader
Business Consultant
Certified Educational Specialist trained by eBay
Member of eBay's Voices of the Community Program

eBay has made creating a business easy. However, designing a successful business model that can grow exponentially is the challenge. I contribute much of the success of Black Knight Trading Company to my son, Joshua Mills. His vision to define the processes and work flows required to "do eBay" long before we became successful have served this company well. It has allowed us to grow from a part-time hobby seller on eBay to a substantial operation with a 9,000 square-foot warehouse and seven employees. Our gross merchandise sales volume has doubled every year for the past five years.

When the founder of eBay, Pierre Omidyar, launched eBay on Labor Day 1995, he had designed it to be self-sustaining. At the time, eBay was not his business; it was his hobby. Understanding there would be times when he would simply not be available, he had the foresight to implement procedures, processes, and flows required to keep his business going in his absence. It is important as you increase your knowledge of eBay to understand the importance of being self-sustaining and educate yourself accordingly.

As Black Knight Trading Company continues to evolve, we have to keep to the principles and ideas of Pierre Omidyar and my son, Joshua. In the summer of this year we will be launching a new software program called "MIA, Manage It Anywhere." It is a Web based application designed to allow any size seller full inventory control and accountability while providing a quick launch multi-channel platform to eBay and other eCommerce sites. You can contact us at **mia@blackknighttrader.com** for information on this exciting new product or the opportunity to become part of our beta testing team.

The ability to define the processes, work flows, and ideas only become apparent after you have a comprehensive understanding of eBay. This book, *eBay's Secrets Revealed* is a tremendous resource in acquiring the necessary knowledge to build a profitable eBay business model. I would be curious to know how much more our income would be today had assets like this book been available when we first started selling on eBay.

eBay's Secrets Revealed will most certainly be on our list of "must reads" for anyone attending any of our "eBay Beyond the Basics" classes or to companies we help with their asset recovery efforts.

INTRODUCTION

eBay has sparked a global revolution in marketing. Anyone with Internet access can start an online business or expand their current endeavor. Whether your attempt is successful depends on your attention to detail in the auction forum and your heeding of the tips in this book to avoid frustration and save precious time and money.

The eBay marketplace is whatever you make of it: a hobby, a livelihood, and even a way of life. But no matter how much you already sell on eBay, odds are you are missing opportunities to maximize your bottom line.

Online auctions offer many handy tools for automation, but they are not advertised or well known, and your competition is not going to alert you online — even inadvertently — to money-saving software and selling tips. Instead of reinventing the wheel, take advantage of the experience of others, explored in this book, to market your product with a minimum of effort.

This book provides an easy reference at each step on your way to the top, and once you get there, how to maintain your status. Whether you wish to create an eBay store, need help with marketing, want to sell internationally, or would like to improve customer service, the fastest route to all of eBay's opportunities is at your fingertips.

The Federal Trade Commission recently reported that the number-one Internet-related complaint is auction fraud scams conducted on eBay and other auction Web sites. Why stumble unknowingly into a legal briar patch when the hazards are clearly marked and the path to success is laid out before you?

A little common sense and honest dealings will get you started, but if you want to be your own boss, increase your visibility, find your niche market, the research has all been done for you. Go ahead, set up your store, process credit card payments, use PayPal confidently, offer coupons, and use cross promotions to up-sell, download digital products, download demographics to profile your customers, and use the same vendor management tools that have made five and dime stores of the 20th Century into mega stores.

Learn how and when to list your items and the best methods for collecting payments. Make the most of headings, keywords, and excellent written descriptions, not to mention the "handling" process. Know when to contact the buyer and when to leave (and expect!) feedback. In addition, there are great tips for getting rid of clutter; taking sharp photos; organizing a filing system of receipts, ideas, and other documents.

Lay a strong foundation for your eBay future by charting your workflow, timetables, deadlines, recurring duties, and most of all, obtain the right hardware and software to manage your space and time. Recognize whether your business idea is sound, perfect your listings, project your income, protect your source of product, and keep the good times rolling by knowing when you need to bring in professional help—a bookkeeper, an attorney, a CPA, or a money manager.

Much of the help you need is right there on eBay, but unless you want to waste valuable time researching, this book gives you access to the entire eBay community of tools, publications, and resources so that you can devote your time to expansion and building awareness of your product.

When you have perused this book and laid out your plans for using everything eBay has to offer, you will be set to take over a category of product on eBay through fast customer service and superior technology.

The eBay Revolution

You may already be operating on eBay, but to be successful you have to get into the belly of the beast and truly understand how it works. Where did eBay come from, what is the company's operating model, and how did they become so successful? eBay, quite simply, provides the infrastructure for entrepreneurs to start their own businesses with very little up-front capital, a concept that has always been attractive to the American psyche, and eBay continues to enhance that infrastructure beyond the basic auction site, with acquisitions like PayPal and Skype.

In the early days of the Internet, owners of small businesses embraced the concept of the virtual store, recognizing that they would be able to compete against much more well-heeled retailers just for the price of some Web hosting. This excitement led many people to exclaim, "I'm going to open up an online store and make big money!" They tried, and most of them failed. The biggest obstacle they faced was that they quickly discovered that online retailing is much like brick-and-mortar retailing, and this basic truth of the retail business guided the online ventures of the future. Some promoters of instant online store sites, drop-shipping vendors, publishers of tutorials, and other purveyors of assorted tools for getting started in online sales, try to create an impression of a business that runs itself. Beware when such a purveyor bandies about phrases like "turnkey operation" and "make money while you sleep." It does not work that way, and running an online business is just as much work as running any other type of business.

The most important truth is that shoppers respond to name recognition. There may be a person on the street selling neckties for $5 apiece around the corner from Macy's, but most of the time, shoppers will pass him by and go into Macy's to buy the same necktie for $50. Now the person with the $5 neckties may have a product that is every bit as good as the $50 neckties inside Macy's, but people gravitate toward recognized names when making transactions. A buyer has no reassurance that the person selling neckties off a table on the street corner has a quality product or that he will still be in business tomorrow. At the same time, the buyer can be reasonably certain that Macy's will still be there. Yes, it would be theoretically possible for me to create an online store called "Dan's Neckties," buy some Web hosting for $5 a month, and go into business, but I would not make many sales. That is where eBay changed the whole dynamic of online retail. Now instead of having an unknown online store called "Dan's Neckties," I can attach my store to something much more recognizable. I can have "Dan's Neckties on eBay." It gives me instant credibility and name recognition.

Where Did It Come From?

The first Internet entrepreneurs out of the gate who had enough business expertise to make some tried business ideas work, created great fortunes. The concept of the electronic marketplace was one of the earliest great ideas, and there are still many of them in existence today. One of the first mass-market e-marketplaces was eBay, also known at first as AuctionWeb.

Being in the right place at the right time accounted for much of the Internet entrepreneurs' success. Like many Internet businesses, eBay started in somebody's living room in Silicon Valley, but unlike most dotcoms, eBay survived and flourished. If eBay founder Pierre Omidyar had come up with this idea ten years later, he would not have succeeded. eBay would have been lost among dozens of other auction sites that would have overshadowed his company. If Mr. Omidyar had not gone down that path in 1995, somebody else would have. It was, in a way, essential for there to be an eBay. There could not be an Internet without an eBay, because (1) he had a great idea, (2) he knew what he was doing, and (3) he was first. eBay has grown to dominate the online auction market today. It has almost become a generic term. There are other auction sites that are just as good technically as eBay, and they charge lower fees for sellers, but eBay has set the standard. "I found 'it' on eBay" is more than just a marketing term used in eBay's television commercials. It reflects the fact that eBay has earned a spot in popular culture. Regardless of whether other auction sites are technically superior, consumers looking for that special, unusual item automatically think of eBay before any other site. Such is the benefit of being the first.

Now, like Mr. Omidyar and other Internet entrepreneurs who came up with that "great idea" of the time, you too, must come up with a great idea. "Selling stuff on eBay" is not great enough. How many times have you heard someone casually say, "I'm going to make some extra money selling stuff on eBay?" It is a statement that far too many people throw around, thinking that it will be easy, thinking that they can make money just by taking a few pictures of junk in the attic and loading them on the eBay site. There is a big difference between those wannabes who always say they need more money and are going to sell "stuff" on eBay, and those people who are determined to start an eBay business. To have a successful eBay business, you too, must come up with a product that fills a need and is better than products anyone else has to offer. You may well start with the junk in your attic, but you cannot end there.

The Business of Selling on eBay

Like any other business, you want to keep your expenses to a minimum, and that is the theme of this book. However, the operative word here is "business." There is a difference between people who "sell stuff on eBay," and people who "have an eBay business." Before we get into the details of operations and keeping down costs, you have to make a decision. Are you just cleaning out your attic, or are you running a business? For those who want to have an eBay business, it is important to realize that there are going to be expenses. You are going to have to put both time and money into the business on an ongoing basis.

The concept of using an online marketplace, whether it is eBay or any other auction or online venue, has brought tremendous efficiencies to businesses and has broadened the marketplace. Now the owners of small businesses can go beyond their communities to market products to the world. While expanded world commerce benefits the buyer, it means more people are marketing the same items in the same way, and the competition is stiffer. In the early days of eBay, there was less competition.

Today it requires constant attention and innovation.

If you approach your eBay activities as a business, there is no limit to what you can do. Make no mistake; most people who sell on eBay make very little money. For the most part, it is because of the simplicity of the eBay model, a plus and a minus. eBay and the Internet have made it remarkably easy to communicate and to attempt to start an online business. The mistake most people make is to believe that because it is easy to get started, it will be easy to keep going. This common misconception causes most online businesses to fail. eBay provides you with the infrastructure. It is up to you to take that and do something with it.

Just because most people fail on eBay does not mean that you are most people. There is a significant minority of eBay folks who are able to earn a respectable second income or even make eBay their primary business. With a little bit of work and some strategic planning you can, too.

The eBay Community

Most eBayers are not big corporations. They are small businesses, part-timers, and people who have brick-and-mortar shops who want to expand their customer base. To an extent, this fact makes the entire eBay community more approachable. After all, it is easier to talk to someone who runs a business out of his garage than it is to talk to the CEO of General Motors, for example.

One of the best ways to build your business is to find out what others who are in the same business are doing. People starting up a large corporation do some intelligence gathering. They may even resort to industrial espionage to find out as much as they can about the competition. They go to meetings of other business people, join associations, and try to schmooze successful people for their secrets.

I have often found that entrepreneurs in general love to talk about their businesses, their success, and how they got where they are today. They are proud of what they have done, and if you ask, they will tell you how they did it. As such, one of the best ways to learn the business is to work your way into the community of other people who are doing the same thing you are. The many eBay forums that exist on eBay's own site is a good place to start.

You will find that eBayers do tend to be a little tighter-lipped than other types of entrepreneurs, and they keep their secrets close. It is a highly competitive marketplace, and although many people succeed, still more fail, and those who do succeed want to continue doing so. On eBay, as with any business, the successful ones do not want to have any more competition than there needs to be. Nonetheless, you will still find valuable information, and people who are willing to talk, and if not share their deepest trade secrets, at least give you some valuable tips and point you in the right direction.

The Internet Revolution and the Dotcom Bust

The eBay revolution goes beyond eBay itself. In fact, the eBay revolution is just one subset of the Internet revolution, which has laid the framework for eBay and many other wonderful opportunities. Even before there was an Internet, the small business community tended to go in cycles. There have been times when small businesses enjoyed more or less success in this country's history. Today consumers tend to prefer large companies, but the Internet presents an opportunity for owners of small businesses. eBay is an infrastructure that lays a framework for other companies. It has allowed the creation of entire cottage industries for thousands of entrepreneurs.

The "dotcom boom" and "dotcom bust" were not the beginning and the end of business on the Internet. There was a brief period where almost anything went, and venture capitalists threw money around like water, but that is over. The subsequent "bust" was really more of a reality check, a move toward a more stable Internet economy. Because of all the media attention on the "dotcom bust," many people think that any dotcom business is doomed. This is not the case. Although the "boom" time created wealth overnight, the dotcom environment today is much more amenable to making money than it was back then. It is more realistic today. We have all had time to sort out what works and what does not. Selling 40-pound bags of dog food on your Web site? Probably not going to work. Selling a hard-to-find collectible? Yes, you have a good chance of making some money.

Robert Sachs, RKS Solutions

Robert Sachs, whose RKS Solutions operates as a liquidator of excess distributor stock via online sales, works with clients to help them eliminate their overstock with the least amount of work on their part. Bob has found a fantastic and lucrative niche in eBay. He notes, "We pick up, inventory and image the stock, create the descriptions and listings, post the items for sale and handle buyer inquiries, handle all payments and packing/shipping issues, and we deliver the net proceeds to our clients via bank checks. We take the stress and work out of selling on eBay."

He adds, "I personally have been performing this consignment sales service for companies in the Memphis area since 1997, with RKS Solutions LLC being formed in February of 2005. We currently are selling an average of $5,000 gross product a month, with both sales count and average price per unit continuing to climb. In 1999 we selected Auction Assistant Pro to be our auction automation solution (now known as Blackthorne Pro)— a choice that continues to provide many benefits for us.

"RKS remains a family business at this time, although we are growing beyond the point of remaining 'all in the family.' We are currently working with other local trading assistants to assist us with handling the growing volume."

CHAPTER 2

Getting Lost

eBay is so large, it is very easy for your items and your eBay store to get completely lost in the shuffle.

Veteran eBayer Robert Sachs (RKS Solutions) has some sound advice to keep from getting lost:

> *"I try to keep my listings clean and easy to read, use a large primary item image (with links to additional images should the buyer want to see more), and keep my terms as simple and compact as possible. I have no gyrating graphics, no irritating sound files, nothing that takes forever to load. Quick, clean, and clear graphics work best for me.*
>
> *Blackthorne Pro has an excellent WYSIWYG (what you see is what you get) auction template editor, allowing me to design and develop very professional auction layouts without having to know much HTML at all. It also allows me to edit the HTML code directly so that I can use features the editor does not support. Over the years, I have developed a style, keeping it fresh with semi-annual updates and minor redesigns."*

Product Selection

The way to avoid getting lost is to not sell something everybody else is already selling. Do what you can to make your listings and your eBay store stand out above thousands of others. If you get an idea to sell a particular item, take a quick look to see how many of them are already on eBay. If there are 1,000 other people already selling the same thing, you are not going to make very many sales. If their search returns a thousand listings, and yours is number 900, chances are, the buyer will never get to your listing, no matter how well you have presented it.

However, if you list something unusual, rare, or in high demand, that only a handful of other eBay vendors are selling, buyers will find your eBay store, no matter what, even if it has a weak design. For example, someone is looking for that unusual product you have listed on eBay. Their search returns five listings, one of which is yours. You have a good chance of making a sale. Dressing up the listing and making it stand out will close the deal.

Do Not Go Overboard

Your job as an eBay entrepreneur includes more than buying and selling. Besides being a skilled strategist, businessperson, and entrepreneur, you also have to be a skilled designer to create an attractive listing. An unskilled designer will resort to garish designs, large arrows and other graphics, and flashing lights. Contrary to what this unskilled designer may think, placing "Look Here!" in huge block letters will not make people look. Remember, not everybody has a powerful computer. Some buyers may have a slow dial-up connection. If your page has intense graphics and too many photos, added music, and dancing logos, it will take too long to load, and they are very likely to wander away before they get a chance to see what you are offering.

On the other hand, your design need not appear bare. The best presentation is one that is balanced — not too sparse and not too busy. Do not feel like you need to fill every inch of your page. Leaving some white space makes the presentation easier on the eye and makes it more attractive.

Look at the excellent auction listings of eBay seller chicshades. The sunglasses he sells are attractive, but what's more important is that the listings are well done. They are not flashy, and his listing design features the sunglasses so that they sell themselves. The text is simple, straightforward, and well organized into separate sections for unhampered reading. Pictures of each pair of sunglasses are Photoshopped (an Adobe program) so that there is no distracting background, and the sunglasses really stand out on the page.

The All-Important Title

Your title should not be an afterthought. Advertising people will tell you the first impression sells, and a good lead-in is what is going to convince people to read the rest of the listing. The title is important because of the way the eBay engine works. Most buyers search titles only when they are looking for something on eBay, so what you put into those few words may decide whether your listing comes up on a search.

1. **You have only 55 characters.** It is important to conserve them. Avoid words like "cool," "great," and "wow." Concentrate instead on words that buyers are likely to include in their search.

2 **Use a combination of upper and lower-case characters.**

Using all capitals does not make your headline any more attention getting. Most people actually find it distracting. Capitalize only one or two important words, not the whole headline.

3 **Do not use asterisks or multiple exclamation points.** It just wastes characters and does not get extra attention.

4 **Do not use abbreviations** because people search on whole keywords.

Keywords

Some shoppers walk into a department store and browse. They walk from floor to floor, sometimes with no direction in mind, just to see what is there. A small online store may work the same way, but eBay is just too big. It is not possible for a shopper to open up eBay on their browser and look through its entire contents. There is too much there. It is search driven. Buyers come to eBay with something specific in mind, and they enter in keywords to find it. Poor use of keywords on the seller's part will result in your listing being completely buried.

When you create a listing, you specify keywords or key phrases. When a potential buyer enters one of the same keywords that you have specified, your listing will come up on their "hit list." Of course, there may be hundreds of others as well, but getting on the buyer's search list is the first step to being seen.

Here is a tip: come up with as many related keywords as you can. Suppose, for example, you have a pearl necklace for sale, and you decide that it is logical to enter in the keyword "pearl necklace." That is obvious, but do not stop there. What if a buyer just enters in the search word "pearls"? Or maybe they will enter in "pearl pendant" or "pearl jewelry."

Search Engine Optimization

The eBay search dialog is not the only place people may be looking for what you have to offer. They may start in the search engines, Google, Yahoo, or MSN, for example, and find a reference to you and be directed to your eBay store.

The subject of search engine optimization is important, and many books are on the market about the subject. I recommend *The Ultimate Guide to Search Engine Marketing: Pay Per Click Advertising Secrets Revealed* by Bruce C. Brown, Atlantic Publishing. The author provides the most current, simple instructions for increasing your profits by advertising on search engines. The important point here is that you want to get your eBay store and your eBay goods listed not just on the eBay search, but on all the other search engines as well.

Submit your eBay store and your "About Me" page to search engines. By far the most important search engine is Google, where most Web surfers go. Open up your Web browser, go to **http://www.google.com/addurl/?continue=/addurl**, and read the information. It is quite simple. All you need to do is type in the URL of your store, follow a few simple instructions, and click the "Add URL" button. Eventually, your store will show up in Google searches, but be patient. Depending on the site and how much traffic it gets, it may take several weeks for it to show up.

Google and other search engines work by indexing your site. Their software, "spider," constantly searches the Web, looking at sites and collecting information about what is on each page. This spider is your friend, and you have to feed it to influence how effective your search strategy becomes. Write to create attractive listings that are descriptive, but also write for the spider. Remember that people will be searching on specific keywords, so use these keywords in your phrasing as often as you can without making it sound awkward. The spider will see these keywords in your text, and will rank their importance. If you use the keyword closer to the top of your text and in your headline, it will be ranked as more relevant. In addition, if you use the keyword multiple times, it will also be ranked as more relevant and, therefore, will show up closer to the top of the search results.

When writing your listings, there are also a few tools to use that will help optimize your listing for search. You may need to know a little bit about HTML, but it is simple. The "META keywords" tag is an HTML tag. The eBay dialog will allow you to enter your own HTML. This is a valuable and often overlooked tool. The META keywords tag will insert keywords into the source code, so search engines can find what you have to sell. The keywords you put into this tag are actually invisible on the page. They are visible only to the spider. Similarly, the "META descriptions" HTML tag is useful in that it displays below the search title in the search results list. This too, is invisible on your site, but it shows up on the results list, so write carefully and descriptively.

A brief review of an introductory HTML tutorial may be in order, but here is what the keyword header looks like for a store that sells pearl jewelry:

<META name="keywords" content="pearls, pearl necklace, pearl jewelry, pearl pendant, black pearls, Japanese pearls, cultured pearls, Mikimoto, baroque pearls">.

Using this META tag, whenever anybody searches on any of the terms included in the tag, your store will show up in the results.

Another tool that some people use in META tags is common

misspellings. It is possible that somebody will conduct a search for "perls", "purls", or "jewlery". You can include these misspelled words in the META tag as well. Do not worry; nobody will see these misspelled words on your page except for the spider!

The description header looks like this:

<META name="description" content="Your complete source for high quality pearl jewelry.">

Using the above tag, the phrase, "Your complete source for high quality pearl jewelry," will appear directly under the title of the page in the search results.

TIP: START SMALL AND BUILD UP

Steven Gardner of Chicshades had some good advice about making a small eBay business into a large one, and he has done quite well in that regard already. "The best advice," he said, "is to start out small and build up your volume at a slow and steady pace. If things get out of hand by having too much volume, you might put yourself in a tricky situation by not being able to fulfill orders and answer e-mails. You also need to learn how to scale your business by using the right set of online selling tools that are available. There are many great eBay books on the market, but I have found the best resources are joining a local eBay group in the area where you live. I also heard from other eBay members that eBay LIVE is a great resource for sellers wanting to make their eBay businesses larger. The eBay message boards are a huge resource and have been a great benefit for me."

Fulfillment

Many online stores fail for several different reasons, but the most frequent one is the lack of a fulfillment strategy. Putting stuff in boxes and taking it to the post office is a time intensive part of your eBay business, but it is one of the most important because it affects your bottom line.

At the beginning, your profit margins may be low. After paying the cost of goods and eBay listing fees, you may be able to reap a 10 percent or 20 percent profit. When you add to those costs, the cost of packaging and shipping, the price of Styrofoam peanuts becomes crucial.

Shipping Is Not a Profit Center

A mistake that some new vendors make is setting a high shipping and handling" fee, based on the logic that time spent packing and traveling to the post office should be worth something. However, they do not charge for answering customers' e-mails, for talking to them on the phone, and for the time spent going to the bank to deposit their checks. Therefore, they should not charge for the time spent going to the post office.

Simply put, you make a profit on your business by setting a price for your goods that takes into account all of your expenses, including the time you spend doing these things. Count on your customers to be wise and cautious. They comparison-shop. They will look at several other vendors who sell the same thing before making a decision, and most of the time they will compare shipping costs as well.

For example, two vendors sell the same product of equal quality. Vendor number one has a price of $20 and vendor number two has a price of $21. Smart shoppers will not assume that the first vendor has the best deal. Instead, they will take a moment to look at the vendors' shipping policies.

If they are shipping a small object via U.S. Postal Service priority mail for $4.35, priority mail shipping boxes and envelopes are available free from the post office meaning that the only shipping expense besides the postage is a couple square feet of bubble wrap. Let's say that the bubble wrap is worth about $.25. Vendor number one has a minimum "shipping and handling" fee of $8, but vendor number two just charges $4.35. If vendor number one gets the order, that vendor will make an extra $3.40, after deducting the priority mail postage and the cost of bubble wrap. Vendor number two just gets back the cost of postage and absorbs the $.25 for bubble wrap. On the surface, it seems as though vendor one would make more money, but in fact, consumers are likely to know the cost of priority mail. They will feel that vendor number one is taking unfair advantage and will go with vendor two, who will make more sales at the end of the day, and have a larger bottom-line profit.

The best strategy for shipping is to break even on your postage and materials. Some large companies offer free shipping with larger orders, which you may consider at some point, but only if you have enough volume to justify the added expense.

TIP: REUSE SHIPPING MATERIALS

In the area of fulfillment, Art and Margo Lemner have a simple approach, first reusing envelopes, shipping boxes, and packing materials from items that have been sent to them, significantly reducing the cost of fulfillment. Their goal is to reduce what they have to charge for shipping, notes Margo, "As that can be a factor, particularly for items with a low selling cost. The post office provides free shipping boxes and envelopes for priority mail, but items less than 13 ounces can go more cheaply first class. Doing a high volume would also reduce the cost, because many packages can go on a single trip to the post office. There are also pickup services if you apply your postage yourself."

Materials

Where you buy your boxes, bubble wrap, labels, and other packing materials can make or break you. Most local department stores or drug stores carry these sorts of items, but if you buy them there, the higher cost will eat into your profit. You must buy in large quantities either from a wholesale supplier or from a large office supply store. Buying one box and a little envelope full of bubble wrap at the drug store will cost ten times more per shipment than if you buy a hundred boxes and a big roll of bubble wrap at your local Office Depot or Staples. You may even be able to get great deals by buying your packing materials directly on eBay from vendors who specialize in providing these sorts of goods.

Constantly re-evaluate your suppliers for these goods and look for bargains. You will have to put out some money ahead of time for a large supply to get a savings. If you just buy a few at a time at the drugstore, your shipping will kill your profits.

Make It Clear

State plainly what your shipping policies are, which shipper you use, and how much you charge. Do not add on extra "handling fees." If enough complaints are filed for "excessive shipping charges," eBay can shut you out.

Make sure your potential customers can see their total cost. Do not surprise them with a high shipping bill. If your shipping fees are not plainly stated and easily understood, you risk having your visitor pass your listing by and going on to the next vendor!

Inventory and Storage

When you are first starting out, keeping track of inventory and storage does not seem to be a big problem, especially if you are only selling a few items. But if your goal is to move far beyond that, it is far too easy to lose track of shipments, send the same thing out twice or not at all, or sell something you no longer have.

Off-site storage has its pros and cons. It may free up space in your home and keep any tobacco smoke, dust, and pet hair out of your packages, but consider the cost of the unit or facility, the cost of travel back and forth, and the inconvenience of being unable to look at a listed item quickly to answer a question about it.

Keeping track of inventory is another must. It is the key to good customer service and efficiency. It avoids mistakes and makes sure customers get the item they bought when they expect it. If you have low volume, you probably do not need any of the expensive and fancy inventory software systems. A set of three by five index cards and pencil is all you need. However, as your business grows, index cards are inadequate. The next step up again can be a simple spreadsheet. Beyond that for high volume sellers, inventory software packages are a good investment.

Prompt Shipping

One of the biggest obstacles in any sort of online sales, eBay or otherwise, is delayed gratification. People love to shop at physical stores, see an item, pick it up, hold it, pay for it, and take it home. They cannot do that at your eBay store. However, your customers will expect to receive their product as quickly as you can get it to them.

Yes, it is a nuisance to make a trip to the post office to mail one item. You may be tempted to "save them up" until you have three or four things to go out. Do not do it! Even if there is only one item, send it out promptly. Whenever possible, ship it out the same day payment is received.

Of course, once you have a large volume, you can avoid trips to the post office altogether by printing your own postage on your computer and scheduling regular pickups of parcels. Besides the post office, FedEx and UPS will also pick up boxes at your home or office if you have an account.

Insurance and Delivery Confirmation

Some sellers insure everything they send out. However, the cost can be significant, especially if you are a high-volume seller. Some sellers find it more economical in the big picture to insure items selectively. When considering insurance, take into account first whether the item is breakable. If it is not, then the only risk against which you are insuring is loss, which seldom happens and will probably cost you more in insurance than your cost of replacement. In other words, taking on the risk yourself instead of buying insurance is probably the best way to go for low value, unbreakable goods. Of course, if an item is breakable or worth more than $100, insurance is necessary.

You may also wish to add "delivery confirmation" to your shipments. In the case of lower value shipments, it tells you that the recipient did indeed receive your shipment.

Outsourcing Fulfillment

Businesses that have very high volumes sometimes outsource the entire fulfillment process, and many have found this to be efficient and cost-effective. However, hiring a fulfillment services company is usually only practical if you have a high volume of goods going out. You will have to figure a break-even point below which it remains better to do it yourself.

Fulfillment centers are able to pack and ship for much less money than you can yourself, because they deal in large volumes. Instead of buying bubble wrap by the carton, they buy it by the truckload, and that makes for some very big cost advantages. Another advantage is that you will not have to run a large warehousing and fulfillment center yourself, and you can keep your actual real estate requirements small. If you have to rent extra space to store and pack your goods, you will lose part of your profit. The final advantage to outsourcing fulfillment is that the provider has an advanced inventory system that will be accurate and speedy. More than likely, your provider will use a bar code system for greater accuracy.

If you do choose to employ a fulfillment contractor, make sure that you are to get regular reports on your activity and that they can handle returns.

One attraction of having eBay businesses is that users can operate out of their homes, and using a fulfillment service allows you to work from home even after your volume grows.

Robert Sachs, RKS Solutions

Bob knows well that fulfillment costs can make or break a business, and he pays close attention to his fulfillment costs. "I selected FedEx for my primary shipping agent based on years of experience with them, comparing rates and service levels to other various carriers. I review my rates on a periodic basis and discuss adjusting them with my FedEx representative, who is very much aware of my business and my needs. I also continue to watch other carriers for products that can lower my costs—like the recent addition of a 'shoe box' sized USPS Priority Mail box. While it only fits about 30 percent of my product line (many of my shoes come in boxes too large for the USPS box), it works very well for the majority of my light items—

sandals, slippers. All packages under two pounds packed weight go USPS Priority Mail, and I make every effort to use the USPS provided box. (It weighs less, requires less void fill, and is FREE.)

"Along that same line, FedEx provides software to produce my FedEx shipping labels and provides the thermal labels suitable for my printer at no cost to me. They even include a cleaning product with each box of labels, helping me to keep my printer in the best condition possible at no additional cost.

"I can also track my costs in Blackthorne—listing shipping charges collected and shipping fees paid. Add to that the cost of purchasing boxes and other supplies and I can easily see if I am losing money or breaking even on shipping. I do not want shipping to become a profit center—I personally do not feel that is good business—but I do expect my shipping charge to cover all of my shipping expenses, from the carrier charges to the boxes and materials and the cost of labor to pack and ship. I am quite happy to break even in that respect.

"Initially I worked with a local small business, a box reseller, to purchase like-new previously used boxes and packing peanuts. When that business closed, the owner was kind enough to point me to his wholesaler, where I now buy my supplies. Since my business is registered with the state of Tennessee, they have no problem selling to me at wholesale prices, even though I am probably one of their smaller buyers."

Your E-mail Ad Campaign

Just creating an eBay store is not enough. You have to let people know it is there, and you have to let your existing customers know that you have more special items for them to buy.

Everyone with an online presence, eBay or otherwise, has to scramble to be noticed. The Internet is expanding by the minute, and an online store that has no promotion will have no customers.

Some sellers are afraid of e-mail ad campaigns and automatically think of "SPAM" when the subject comes up. That is because a handful of unethical marketers blanket the Internet with millions of ads promoting low-value products. Because they can send out millions of e-mails inexpensively, they still make money even if they get a very low response. They do get an abysmally low response rate and also run the risk of angering customers, getting shut down by their ISP, or even violating the law.

Nobody wants to be accused of sending SPAM, and the fear of

such an accusation is so great that many vendors avoid e-mail campaigns altogether. However, remember this: Not all e-mail ad campaigns are SPAM. It is profitable to conduct a legitimate, non-SPAM e-mail ad campaign. In fact, an opt-in e-mail advertising campaign, as opposed to a SPAM campaign, will yield much better results every time.

You can build your own permission-based or opt-in e-mail marketing by either building your own opt-in list or purchasing one. Third party companies compile opt-in lists for sale, typically offering recipients some sort of award or incentive, such as earning points toward discounts or free goods. Offering an incentive is a great way to build your own list as well.

If you buy an opt-in list, research the vendor before you buy. Find out how they get people to opt-in, what incentives they offer, and how often the list is used. If the opt-in list is overworked, it will be useless. Also, find out details about targeting. A vendor who gets opt-in customers with simple techniques like "Click here to receive offers from our partners and get a free gift" will not have a high quality customer list. One that surveys the specific interests of their opt-in customers will generate a higher quality list and will be able to sell you a subset of their list that contains names of individuals that have expressed an interest in products that you offer.

Here Are a Few Simple Do and Do Not Rules

1. Do not buy bulk mailing lists.

2. Do include useful information in your e-mails, such as informative articles and tips.

3. Do include an "opt-out" with your e-mails so that recipients can opt to not receive them.

4. Do include an "opt-in" with your orders so that your customers can receive your e-mail promotions.

5. Do not send out e-mail promotions too often. Once month is more than enough.

6. Do not include attachments in your e-mails. People will suspect that they are trojan programs and will not open them.

7. Do not post self-promoting entries to newsgroups or forums.

8. Do give recipients of your e-mails something "extra," such as a special price or discount.

A good e-mail campaign is one of the most effective, inexpensive ways of promoting your eBay store. Do not be afraid to use it.

Customer Mailing List

As any successful e-mail marketer will tell you, the highest returns come from repeat customers. One way to encourage repeat business is by maintaining a mailing list of your customers.

Your customers are valuable to you, so do not overdo it. Treat them with respect. Do not send out too many e-mails and offer them something of value when you do e-mail, such as an informative article or a "good customer" discount offer.

You can use any one of several available third-party mailing list packages or services, but for most purposes your eBay store features will be all you need. Depending on the type of store you have, you may send a certain number of free e-mails every month, and you pay only a small fee if you exceed the free threshold. Using the free e-mails is the easiest way to manage an eBay mailing list because it is integrated right in your store tools from the "Manage My Store" menu. You can also use "Outlook" to manage your e-mail lists, a handy program that most people already have installed.

Your eBay Store Newsletter

An e-mail should be more than just a brief note that says you have something for sale. Newsletters have become very popular and are often quite successful, because they go beyond being a mere advertisement. A newsletter written in an inviting tone is fun, informative, and more likely to be read. Customers will recognize it and look forward to it every month.

Besides the obvious promotional information describing what you have to offer this month, your newsletter should include informative articles that are relevant to your product line. For example, if you sell fishing lures, include articles about fishing.

By making it useful, you can turn subscribers into customers. You can create a small ad on your eBay store to promote your newsletter and allow people to sign up. You can do this easily in the "Manage My Store" dialogue through the "Promotion Boxes" feature.

The tone of your newsletter should be professional, yet friendly and conversational. It should be attractive and well laid out, but not too flashy. Almost anybody can create a newsletter with existing tools on most computers, but not everybody should. A poorly designed and poorly written newsletter is worse than no newsletter at all and will kill your business very quickly. If you are not skilled in this regard, consider hiring a professional writer or newsletter company to do it for you. One place to find skilled writers is on Elance **www.elance.com**, an e-marketplace primarily used to match up service providers with business owners who need their particular skills.

"Opt-In" E-Mails

The most basic rule of e-mail marketing is to use an "opt-in" policy, which allows your customers and potential customers to agree ahead of time to receive your e-mails or newsletters. You can do this with a simple promotional box that advertises your newsletter or offers something like, "click here to receive information about our special offers." You can also use eBay's tools to include an opt-in invitation whenever you send out any correspondence. In addition, you should consider every customer interaction as an opportunity to add to your list, even if a person is only making an inquiry. Similarly, if you have another online store, you can solicit visitors there to opt-in as well. If you have a brick-and-mortar store, or even sell on weekends at a flea market, always carry a clipboard and a sign-up sheet with you. You would be surprised how many people will write down their e-mail addresses if they like what they see.

By all measures, marketing campaigns that are targeted at opt-in lists receive a far greater positive response than those that do not, and nobody can call it SPAM. An opt-in e-mail campaign is legitimate.

It is against eBay policy for you to send e-mails to customers who have not opted-in to your marketing program. eBay also limits the number of your e-mail campaigns to once weekly, and this is more than adequate. In most cases, once a month is optimal.

HTML Versus Text

E-mails were once simple, text-based affairs. If you wanted to add attention to a particular word, you would put asterisks on both sides of it or maybe capitalize it. An e-mail newsletter was very plain with layout limited to what could be done with plain text formatting. It was functional, but it was no match for the flashy graphics of the print magazine.

That did not last long. Easy HTML tools have made it possible to create flashy e-mails with assorted fancy fonts, graphics, and embedded pictures. Studies show that an HTML-based, lightly graphic e-mail marketing messages get better results, but there are a few caveats and rules to follow. It can certainly be overdone with flash. Keep it simple. Even if you include no graphics at all, an HTML e-mail can still be attractive just with varied font styles and sizes and some embedded links that can take your viewer directly to your offering page on the Web. Of course, HTML e-mails give you many other practical uses beyond presentation.

For example, a non-embedded graphic can be added for letting you know whether each individual e-mail was opened.

Some marketers prefer to include a check box at the opt-in menu, which gives users the choice between text-based and HTML-based messages. While most people today have no objection to receiving HTML e-mails, a few do. For example, people whose computers are slow prefer text-based e-mails for performance purposes. Sight-impaired people may prefer text-based e-mails because it works better with special voice software they use for reading.

When creating your e-mail message or newsletter, brevity is also important, since people tend to get bored with long e-mails. If your message must be several pages long, include a summary of the story in the e-mail with an attractive headline and a link to the full article on a separate Web site. Before you send out an HTML e-mail marketing campaign, e-mail it to yourself, to run a simple test to make sure that there are no broken links or bad graphics.

The eBay Stores E-Mail Marketing Program

In most cases, it is going to be easier and cheaper to manage your e-mail marketing campaign with tools you already have access to, rather than acquiring something extra. Fortunately, you get several useful tools along with your eBay store that you can use. Your eBay Stores e-Mail Marketing Program is one such tool, and you can use it to create and manage your e-mail marketing campaigns.

You can use this tool to create graphically rich e-mails that include text and pictures of featured "for sale" items and other graphics. Be sparing with your use of graphics. Graphically rich HTML-based e-mails do get better responses, but e-mails that are too heavy will bog down computers that do not have broadband. Limit the number of graphics you use in these e-mails to two or three. The eBay tool also has convenient and attractive templates to make it easy to create attractive messages; or if you prefer, you can create your own HTML. The utility will also give you some useful information and allow you to keep track of how many recipients you sent the e-mails to, how many actually opened it, and how many clicks resulted.

> *Of course, it takes more than good product to drive repeat business. Steven knows this well, and he orchestrates his own e-mail marketing campaigns. He uses the Constant Contact e-mail marketing program and this drives a significant amount of repeat business for him. He also cross-markets his own e-commerce site via eBay and his other eBay seller ID. He adds, "I used to pay for Yahoo keywords and Google paid advertising, but I find it to be too costly at this point."*
>
> **-Steven Gardner, Chicshades**

Robert Sachs, RKS Solutions

Bob Sachs, whose RKS Solutions operates as a liquidator of excess distributor stock via online sales, works with clients to help them eliminate their overstock with the least amount of work on their part. Bob has found a fantastic and lucrative niche in the eBay world by offering a service that helps others. In describing what he does, Bob notes, "We pick up, inventory, and image the stock, create the descriptions and listings, post the items for sale and handle buyer inquiries, handle all payments and packing/shipping issues, and deliver the net proceeds to our clients via bank check. We take the stress and work out of selling on eBay."

He added, "I personally have been performing this consignment sales service for companies in the Memphis area since 1997, and RKS Solutions LLC was formed in February of 2005. We currently are selling an average of $5,000 gross product a month, with both sales count and average price per unit continuing to climb. In 1999 we selected Auction Assistant Pro to be our auction automation solution (now known as Blackthorne Pro) – a choice that continues to provide many benefits for us. "

Inventory

Acquiring items for your eBay business may be the most fun, but once you get all those goods home, what do you do with them until they are sold?

Running a business out of one's home is wonderful. I have been working at home for 15 years, and a few of those years were spent selling imported goods. Most of my work now involves writing, and this activity does not take up very much space. The difference between the two is clutter.

Homes are just not designed to double as warehouses. However, if you want to sell on eBay and you want to work at home, as most eBay folks do, you have to make do and carve out some space. Ideally, you have a large house and can devote one entire room to your eBay business. There is something unsettling about having stacks of computers and books in one's living room.

Large companies handle inventory on an automated basis. Goods are logged into a computer when they come in, affixed with a bar code, and stocked on shelves that are arranged in a particular order. When an order comes in, a picker armed with a bar code reader will take the items off the shelf, and the bar code reader automatically takes it out of inventory. Ideally, the inventory system is also integrated with billing and accounts receivable, so that a bill can automatically be generated. It is also integrated with the ordering system so that when a particular item gets low in stock, an order can be generated for more. But these sorts of systems take up a great deal of space and are expensive, and for a small eBay operation selling a hundred pieces a week, you probably do not need it. You do, however, need some sort of inventory control system.

Crash and Burn

It is often said that the most successful entrepreneurs are also the biggest failures.

It is inevitable that some businesses will fail. When a business, or a specific product line, ends up not making you any money or worse, costing you money—do not give up. That is the biggest mistake an entrepreneur can make. Make your mistakes and move on to the next idea. Successful entrepreneurs are not necessarily any more savvy than anybody else. They are just too stubborn to quit.

Inventory control can make the difference between success and failure. Without an adequate system, you will make mistakes, get negative feedback, and lose customers. Businesses fail that do not adjust to success. Constant review and upgrade of your inventory control system is essential for continued success.

"Where Is An Item" Feature

A useful inventory tool you get with your eBay store is eBay's own "Where Is an Item" function. While this does not help you figure out which closet you stuck it in, it does help you figure out where it is in the virtual eBay world. Using this feature, you can get a listing of each item you have on sale, and under which category it is listed.

It easy to get out of sync between what's on eBay and what you actually have on hand, especially if you are managing hundreds of items at once and have perhaps more than one sales outlet. Suppose, for example, you remember at midnight that it is your sister's birthday tomorrow, and you do not have time to go to the store—but you remember that cute necklace that you have listed and you think she would like it. You take it out of stock, wrap it up, and bring it over to the party. But the next day, after you have already given it away, you discover that somebody has bid on it. Now you are in big trouble. You either have to do a disservice to a potential customer and tell them they cannot have the item, or ask your sister to give it back. Either way, you are in the doghouse.

Standard procedure should be to remove an item from your eBay listings the minute you take it out of stock and to run the "Where Is an Item" report periodically to perform a routine crosscheck to make sure that you still have everything available that you are listing.

What to Sell?

The key to success is flexibility. eBay stores that sell one or two items exclusively may do very well for a time but will run out of steam before long. Do not be afraid of trying something new. eBay seller Robert Sachs (RKS Solutions) relates his own experience in broadening his inventory and achieving Powerseller status simply by keeping an open mind and being willing to expand into new territory.

"My inventory has come to me primarily through two channels my listing in the eBay Trading Assistant directory, and via word-of-mouth as my current clients share their experiences with others.

"I've recounted the tale of signing our primary client many times: I received a call from a gentleman looking to dispose of some old personal electronics—an older computer, some stereo equipment. He found my trading assistant listing on eBay and wanted to know if I was interested. I was not. There was nothing in the list worth the effort of providing my services, but a little voice asked me what else did I have going? I had been laid off (after 25+ years as an IT consultant) nine months earlier and things were still slow. So I agreed to meet with him and look over his stuff.

"After spending a few minutes in his waiting area, I was getting a good idea of the business his company was in, but when I entered his office I found out he was a vice president of the company. We discussed his personal items, agreed on the terms, and I then handed him a copy of my standard consignment contract for his information. He asked if I needed a copy for my files. I informed him that for these few personal things, I did not need the contract, but that if I were to begin selling for his company, we'd have one.

"You could literally see the bulb light up. He had never considered using eBay for his company's products! We toured the warehouse where he showed me a large collection of overstock items, odd bits of inventory left after big shipments went out or that were returned from various retail outlets when product lines were discontinued. They either donated these items to a local charity (which they continue to do today) or they destroyed them and wrote them off the books. Did I think I could sell any of them?

"I didn't recognize most of the brands. What do I know about women's shoes? But I accepted a few pair of dress and athletic shoes. A week later I came back for more, and within 30 days I was selling over a dozen pair of shoes every week. Within two months I had made it to Bronze PowerSeller ($1,000 a month average gross product sales over the last three months), and moved up to Silver about a year later ($3,000 a month average sales).

"I also continue to buy small lots of miscellaneous computer-related items for resale. Even thought I started with them, these sales represent less than 5 percent of my total sales."

A key point is to avoid being stuck on one particular item. Products naturally go through a cycle, and sales of any given item or category will fluctuate for any number of reasons. Sales of something may go well for a while, but a store chain may start carrying the same item at a discount price, to your dismay.

Here is a brick-and-mortar example that also holds some truth for the eBay world. When my wife and I were running an import shop, we were bringing in exotic goods from the Orient and selling them at boutique prices. About six months later, dollar store chains started bringing in the same things and selling them at dollar store prices. Sales dropped, and we got out of the import business.

The point is to remain flexible in your product line and do not be afraid to move to new items. Watch your sales patterns carefully and keep an eye on your competition. Your success on eBay hinges on the rarity and cost.

> ## TIP: WOULD YOU BUY IT?
>
> *Do not sell anything you wouldn't buy for yourself or your family. You would not want to get stuck with junk and neither will your buyers. And it's easier to make a repeat sale to a satisfied customer.*
>
> **- Robert Sachs, RKS Solutions**

Avoid Narrow Focus

If you have been selling a particular item successfully, you may be tempted to think that if you can sell ten of them a week, why not try to list a hundred. It does not always work that way. Putting more of any one product on the eBay market will only drive down the price—which is good for the buyers, but not so good for you.

Instead of trying to sell thousands of a single item, branch out. It is okay to keep your items in the same category, and in fact, doing so will help give you some name recognition as the "expert" in that category but try to accumulate and offer several different products in a category. A good product mix is vital to retail success, whether you are online, on eBay, or running a corner store. A mix will enhance your opportunity for cross-sell and up-sell. If you have a customer who buys one item and you have other related items, you have a chance of making more sales to a customer.

Arthur and Margo Lemner,

"To avoid receiving negative feedback, many sellers put information on their auctions or their follow-up e-mails after the sale that tells the buyer to contact them to resolve any problems before leaving feedback. That is eBay's preferred method of resolving conflicts, as misunderstandings can easily arise. Sometimes a buyer will make mistaken assumptions about an auction item based on too little information. Therefore, it is a good idea for sellers to be as complete as possible in describing their items. Also, buyers need to ask any possible questions they can think of before bidding.

"If the person you are dealing with is not reasonable, you may receive negative feedback through no fault of your own. Also, if you have to leave negative feedback because the other party is not being honest, they may retaliate with negative feedback. If your feedback rating is high enough, a few negatives will not have a great impact, and it is important to warn others about the problem eBay user. Therefore, I won't hesitate to leave negative feedback if it is deserved. There is a process by which you can add your own short comment in response to a negative feedback, giving you a chance to tell your side of the story. Unfortunately, sellers with very high feedback can be rather arrogant and not treat a customer fairly if there is a problem. You can usually tell from their comments in a negative feedback that they have a major attitude problem."

Payments

I knew one eBay seller who insisted that all buyers pay by money order no PayPal, no checks, no credit cards just snail-mail money orders. Later on, he decided to accept checks but then insisted on waiting two weeks before shipping for the check to clear.

By insisting on narrow payment methods, he eliminated about 90 percent of his potential customers. Today you must offer a highly desirable item for this strategy to work.

It is true that you do have to worry about security and fraud, but you also have to offer good customer service. Two things worked against the seller I mentioned:

1. **Customers** do not like to wait for their products.

2. **Customers** do not like to go to any extra trouble to buy what they want.

No doubt, you will lose customers if you require them to take extra steps or make them wait for two weeks while their check clears the bank. Yes, those are policies that guarantee you payment security, but they are not practical.

If you do receive a paper check in the mail, it is probably not necessary to wait ten days before shipping. That used to be the case, but banking has changed. Since the "Check 21" law was passed by Congress, banks are now able to exchange checks electronically. Since banks do not have to send paper checks between themselves, checks clear faster than ever. "Seven to ten working days" used to be the rule, but now, that is excessive. When you deposit a check, most banks clear it within one or two days. Check with your bank to make sure of their policies. You may also wish to use a check verification service, which will ensure that a check is good immediately.

Naturally though, you want your customer to pay before you send the goods. Although, I have also met a few who have erred on the other side of the spectrum as well, and sent out goods with nothing more than an invoice and trust in humankind. These people lose out in the end. The simple solution is in the middle:

1. Get your money before shipping

2. Make it easy for customers to pay

3. Ship out goods as soon as payment is received

4. Make it clear how much is owed

Let your customers make their purchases immediately and pay for them as soon as their bid is accepted. The more time that elapses between the time a customer decides, "Yes, I want that," and the time when he makes his payment, the less likely it is that the transaction will ever be completed. If they have to go out and buy a money order, they will be put off. "I'll pick up the money order when I go out tomorrow," they think to themselves, but it gets put off and time passes, and eventually they abandon their purchase altogether.

PayPal

PayPal, which eBay owns, is one of the most common ways of accepting payment from your sellers. By opening up a business account with eBay, your customers can pay you out of their PayPal account balances or can simply use their credit or debit cards.

Just maintaining a personal PayPal account is not enough if you are a merchant. You cannot accept credit card payments with a personal account, but the business account lets your customers pay for items right away with very little trouble.

Naturally, there is a fee involved for each transaction, but this would be true for any type of credit card merchant account as well. PayPal, since it is part of eBay, integrates very well with eBay, and it has a "Winning Buyer Notification Feature" that will automatically forward a request for payment to the winner of each of your auctions. This feature in itself is quite valuable, since it saves you from having to request payment manually every time and makes sure it gets done right away.

Some people take exception to using PayPal for one reason or another. They may be concerned about security, although PayPal is just as secure as any other form of electronic funds transfer, and the company has taken some major steps to ensure against fraud. It is a safe way to transfer money. There are those, nonetheless, who do not like some of PayPal's policies, and there are numerous Web sites devoted to those who dislike them. However, most of your customers will want to pay you with PayPal, so you are advised to sign up for it or risk losing business.

PayPal Is Not a Bank

You should be aware that although it operates like one, PayPal is not a bank. Therefore, it is not subject to the same regulations as a bank, a point of some concern. PayPal can do things that banks cannot do, such as freeze your account under certain circumstances. Because of this organizational distinction, it is wise not to keep money in your PayPal account. Withdraw it regularly and put it into your normal bank account. PayPal is a vehicle for moving money back and forth. It is not designed to be a savings account, so do not use it like one.

Escrow Service

You can use an escrow service to collect payment, and this ensures legitimacy on both sides. However, this is meant only for large purchases. If you insist on escrow for smaller purchases, buyers will not want to go to the trouble, and again, you will lose some business.

For purchases of say, $500 or more, escrow works quite well. An escrow service is a third party trusted company, which holds the payment until the buyer receives and approves the merchandise. This way, you, the seller, know that the buyer has made the payment in good faith (even though you do not have it in your hands yet), and you can feel free to send out the goods without fear of non-payment. The buyer also knows that the goods have been sent out, and there is some recourse if they are not received or are substandard.

Money from a Foreign Country

For most ordinary, small-item auctions, it is better to limit your auction to buyers in your own country. The extra steps required in payments and customs are just more trouble than it is worth to sell a $10 item to someone in Padua when you live in Pittsburgh.

However, there may be circumstances when you want to open up an international auction. If you have a very high-value collector's item that is worth tens of thousands of dollars, it may be worth the effort to sell worldwide.

If you accept payments in PayPal, you are able to accept not only U.S. dollars, but also Canadian dollars, Japanese Yen, British Pound Sterling, and Euros. While the figure should be based on the exchange rate at the time of payment, be aware that exchange rates vary frequently, and by the time you receive payment, you may actually gain or lose a small amount. Larger international companies absorb these amounts, sometimes actually finding a small profit in the exchange. However, do be aware that the protections that PayPal offers through its PayPal Seller Protection Policy do not apply to international sales.

You will also have no protection against fraudulent chargeback schemes. An international buyer can easily tell PayPal that they did not receive the goods, and you may have no way to prove otherwise. Your account will be charged, and you will be out of luck. For this reason, some sellers limit overseas buyers to paying through Western Union or bank checks.

Then there is Customs, meaning extra paperwork. You will need to describe precisely the contents of the package. Your customer may have to pay a customs tax on their end, based on the type of goods that you are sending; therefore, you must be accurate.

In our import business, the customs tax we paid varied and was dependent on how accurate our person in Bangkok was in filling out the forms. Receiving a box of plastic chopsticks costs one rate, and a box of wooden chopsticks costs another. You must specify not only the goods, but also their composition. If it is clothing, you must specify the material: a cotton skirt or a silk shirt, not just a skirt or a shirt. Do not try to do your buyer a favor by listing a price that is undervalued, even if they request that you do that so they will pay a lower customs fee. Doing so is illegal. If you sell high-value items, it may be worthwhile to use the services of a customs broker to handle the paperwork for you.

Even Receiving Money Costs Money

All of these services cost you money. When figuring your pricing, the cost of receiving funds is one of the costs that many beginners forget to factor in. If your profit margin is slim, the money you spend on PayPal fees, escrow services, customs brokers, and other such things can turn your profit into a loss very quickly. Keep careful track. Make it clear ahead of time who pays for things like escrow fees so that there is no dispute.

Another tactic that some sellers use (and most buyers dislike) is to add a surcharge for credit card purchases to cover the service charge. "If I take credit cards, I have to pay extra," the beginning eBay merchant reasons. "So I should pass that on to the customer." The beginning merchant believes that since he or she is allowing a customer to use a credit card, it is okay to charge for that service.

Never do this! It may make perfect sense to you, but buyers just want to pay in whatever way is easiest for them. The fees that you are charged by PayPal and credit card companies are your cost of doing business, and you have to absorb them and just figure them into your overall pricing strategy. Adding surcharges for any other reason will cost you business.

Accounting and Taxes

If you are starting a business, that means recording some numbers. You will need to keep track of every penny you spend and make for the tax man and for yourself. You need to see where your money is going, which items are selling during which seasons, and whether you are turning a profit.

Beginners think that they will know automatically whether they are turning a profit. When they see money in their pocket, they think they are turning a profit, but that is not always the case. Their profit is often not as large as they think it is, or it may not exist at all.

Accounting Systems

Most eBay merchants want to use a computer-based program.

This does not necessarily mean that you have to spend hundreds of dollars for an accounting package. For basic needs, the programs you already have on your computer may suffice. If you have a basic knowledge of accounting, you can do everything you need with a spreadsheet program that you probably already have on your computer.

Accounting packages specially designed for small businesses are easy to run. Accounts and procedures are set up in default systems, and all you have to do is enter the numbers. They are designed for non-accountants.

Accountants and CPAs

Accountants and CPAs will prove to be very valuable associates for you, and their services will be well worth the money. However, there are two ways to use their services: the first is simply to save all the scraps of paper and receipts, put them in a shoebox, and send them over to the accountant's office. He will sort it out, but you will be charged for the service.

The second, and most logical approach, is to think of the accountant as a partner who refines what you have already done. Get all of your accounts and paperwork organized ahead of time. Enter in your sales and expenses in a logical way in a spreadsheet or a simple accounting package, and present it to your accountant, who generates monthly sales and expense reports that show you how your business is doing.

The accountant will also take care of some of the more complicated things, like taxes and payroll. He or she will be familiar with the forms you must file with government agencies and will make sure you file them on a timely basis to avoid penalties.

Goals

One may think of setting financial goals for your eBay business as part of the "inspirational" section of the book, but it belongs in the accounting section just as easily. Establishing a financial goal for your business does require inspiration and belief in yourself, but carrying out that goal requires strict attention to the numbers. You will not achieve it if you do not pay attention to the numbers on paper.

Publicly traded companies have very strict goals. The performance of the stock market depends on those goals. Every quarter, companies set forth guidance for investors to predict how the companies will perform in the coming quarter and fiscal year. If the company does not meet that guidance, the price of the stock goes down. So for these companies, it is more than just an airy prediction. A great deal rides on setting and achieving those goals every quarter. Of course, you are an eBay merchant and not a publicly traded company, but the same principles apply. Set your goals and work to achieve them.

Goals must be very specific and measurable. Simply having a goal of "selling more on eBay this quarter" is not enough. Instead, set a specific goal: "Increase sales by 10 percent this quarter over last quarter." You can measure that in hard numbers and see your success on paper. Write out specific plans and steps such as creating more attractive auction listings.

How much money do you want to make? How much do you need? These simple questions form the basis of your goal. Suppose for example, you earn $3,000 a month at your day job, and you want to earn that much from your eBay business so you can quit that job. That is your first goal. Now you need to figure out how to achieve it, which means deciding how many items you have to sell and at what profit.

Return on Investment

Accounting means calculating your return on investment and your profit margin. Over the course of your eBay business or any business for that matter, you will put money into that business. You will buy software, hire employees, contract for services, and rent office space. It is not always easy to predict an exact figure for return on investment (ROI) for every expenditure, but you can get a good idea of whether it is a good investment. Analyze all of your investments periodically. You may find that you are spending money every month on something that does not give you a significant return.

> ## EXAMPLE:
>
> *I have a fax machine in my home office, and without plugging in exact numbers I know that the $100 I spent on it was a wise investment. I do not send or receive faxes often, but when I do, it saves me time and money by not having leave the house. For a while, I had a second phone line installed and tied directly to my fax machine. This added the small convenience of having the fax machine on line at all times, but I had to pay for a second phone line. When I analyzed it, the line was not necessary.*

You will total all the expenses a product incurs, weigh that against the selling price, and derive a ratio. If you sell $1,000 worth of products and you spent $750 to acquire them, you feel good about it and figure you are making about 25 percent. But wait. Adding up the amount you spent to acquire the products, the price of your eBay listings, your PayPal fees, shipping expenses, and packing gives you a gross profit margin of about 10 percent.

However, you are not done. There are indirect expenses. You add the amount you spend on rent, advertising, and office supplies, and you have another $200. That means you are $100 in the hole with a net profit of minus 10 percent.

Legal Structures

Also under the purview of accounting comes the legal structure of your business. Again, if you are just selling a few odd items and do not have much volume, you do not need to worry too much about this. But you are reading this book, and that means you want more success than that, and your eBay business is going to become significant. It is time to start thinking about formalizing your business and making it a distinct entity.

Formalizing your company into either a corporation or registering it as a proprietorship will have another benefit. It will give you and your business a greater air of legitimacy. This is handy not only in dealing with customers and putting on a professional face, but it is also useful when dealing with the IRS.

Deductions

Naturally, if you were making money, even a small amount, the IRS wants their share. It is up to you to keep your books up to date and make sure that you are taking all the deductions to which you are legally entitled.

Part of figuring those deductions is determining, from the IRS's point of view, whether your eBay operation is a legitimate business or just a hobby. That is a big argument in favor of imposing a legal structure, such as that of a corporation, onto your business. Seek out an accountant to advise you on the specific structure that works best for you. Do not assume that you need to be a corporation to be legitimate. You do not. You can still be a sole proprietor and be considered a professional business, so long as you act like a business.

You do not want the IRS to think your eBay business is a hobby, because that limits what you can deduct. If you are an eBay hobbyist, you do not file a Schedule C (business income and deductions). Your eBay-related expenses would only be lumped into your standard deduction.

There is really no hard and fast IRS rule for what is a hobby and what is a business, but generally, if you are making money at it, you are a business. Be sure to report all of your income, list all of your expenses, and try your best to make sure that the expenses deducted do not exceed your income. If that is the case, you are in serious trouble and need to re-think your strategies.

Having a home office is not only a great way to work. It is also a great tax deduction. So long as you run your business primarily out of your home and you have a dedicated space in your home for that business, you can take the home office deduction.

A quick look at Chicshade products shows some high-quality goods at reasonable prices, yet Steven said that his profit margin continues to be great. "I believe it also has to do with how you market your product. My average markup for most of my items is ten times my initial investment." He describes his pricing strategies as having two components, one for auctions, and another for "Buy It Now" items. "For the most part, all my auction listings start just under $10. On some occasions I will increase the price depending on items that I am selling. For "Buy It Now" items, I increase the price by usually $5.

-Steven Gardner, Chicshades

Preventing Fraud

The Internet has brought us many wonderful things and many great opportunities for entrepreneurship. But for almost as long as the Internet has existed in a commercial sense, there has been fraud. Crooks, con artists, and thieves see the Internet as a perfect opportunity for illicit gain, and some of them have been wildly successful, taking millions of dollars in various cyber schemes, identity theft strategies, and online swindles.

In addition, if you have a romantic idea about computer hackers that they try to break into computers just for the challenge and intellectual stimulation, think again. These guys are not idealists who want to make social statements. They are not doing it out of boredom, and they are not misunderstood geniuses. They are crooks. Moreover, while in the early days of the Internet, there may have been some who broke into computers as a hobby, those types of hackers today are rare. Today's hackers are criminals who want to take your money. A great deal of money moves back and forth on eBay, so it is a natural target.

Acceptable Loss

Naturally, you will want to take as many steps as possible to prevent fraud, but any large business will experience some loss, regardless of the steps they take to prevent it. Bean counters who keep track of large retail chain stores determine what is an "acceptable rate of loss" to the corporation. They realize that it is inevitable and setting an expectation of acceptable loss will provide a framework for how much money you should spend on fraud prevention and what you should expect.

eBay Powerseller Steven (chicshades) offers his insight into making sure you do not fall victim to a fraud but acknowledges that every eBayer must realize that there is a certain level of acceptable loss:

> *"As an eBay seller you will be sure to fall victim of this scam if you ship internationally and you ship parcel post. Since there is no tracking on this type of shipping you cannot be certain an overseas buyer has or has not received his or her product. The scam works that the buyer has received the item, but files a PayPal claim stating the item has not been received and does a chargeback. The result is the buyer gets his product and his money back. That is, if they paid for the item using PayPal. This has happened to me twice so far, but it is a small price to pay when doing business on eBay."*
>
> **-Steven Gardner, Chicshades**

Spending time and money on fraud prevention is a part of business, and you should expect to have to do so. Keep in mind that there is a decreasing rate of return, and most security experts will acknowledge this general fact of business. For example, suppose you put in a few hours a week in fraud prevention efforts and add a few extra steps to your selling procedures. You spend a few hundred dollars on fraud prevention software and take the extra precaution of getting a "return receipt" when you send items via USPS. These small steps will give you big returns in terms of fraud and loss prevention.

Suppose then, that after taking these steps, you see one or two items a month disappearing because of fraud. You must then decide whether that is acceptable or step up your loss prevention efforts. Stepping up your efforts may result in lower loss rates, but it can have other consequences as well. For example, you may decide to take the extra measure of never accepting checks and charging extra shipping fees so you can insure every item. You also decide to refuse to ship parcel post, even though it offers the customer a lower shipping rate because it cannot be tracked. By taking these extra steps, you must now weigh your decreased loss rate against the fact that you will lose some customers who want to pay by check or who want to buy items only from merchants who offer the lowest shipping rates.

The bottom line here is that you should do everything you can to prevent fraud, but it is just not realistic to expect that it will never happen to you.

Supplier Scams

There are many different types of fraud out there. While you may associate fraud with either sellers who are selling non-existent or substandard goods or with buyers who attempt to defraud sellers out of their products or payments, it goes beyond that.

When you are running a successful eBay business, one of your biggest concerns is obtaining goods, and this too, is an area of concern.

When you start to look for something to sell, you will encounter many great deals, many of them legitimate, but you will also encounter some bogus claims. Never take suppliers at their word and do as much due diligence as possible before buying. The Web is full of suppliers, wholesalers, drop-shippers, and others who offer fabulous, unheard-of deals, but many of these sources are worthless. The products may look good in the picture on your computer monitor, but when you get them in the mail, they may be cheaply made imitations of the real thing that are barely worth what you paid for them. The only way you could sell them for a profit is to perpetrate the same fraudulent claims the supplier made to you.

That is not to say that you should not buy wholesale goods online. After all, online commerce is what your eBay business is built on. Just beware of the risks, do some research, and ask if you can order just one item as a sample before you commit to a whole case load of something.

A few simple guidelines to go by when looking for online wholesale suppliers:

- Beware of outrageous claims of high profits.

- Never buy from a supplier that does not include contact information and a physical address.

- Be very cautious of buying supplier lists. (They are usually worthless, and you can get the same information yourself on the Web for free.)

- Avoid multi-level marketing schemes.

- Look for a supplier with a good track record and references.

- Suppliers should have a readily-accessible help desk or support call number.

- Samples of products should be available for free or for a small fee.

Similarly, counterfeit goods are rampant in online marketplaces, and you can get yourself into serious trouble trying to buy and sell them, even if you do not realize they are counterfeit. Use some common sense. If a supplier is selling Prada handbags for $5 apiece, they are probably counterfeit.

If you do deal in high-end, designer items, do be aware that virtually every expensive designer item has a counterfeit equivalent somewhere in the world. I have personally seen the counterfeit $5 Prada handbags for sale in a bazaar in Southeast Asia, and they looked realistic. (I avoided the temptation of bringing home a suitcase full of them.) Before you deal in any type of high-end, designer item, learn to tell the difference between the real thing and a fake.

Delivery Confirmation

When you send items via the U.S. Postal Service, the cheapest fraud prevention you can get is delivery confirmation. For 50 cents, you can have some assurance that your package arrived at its destination and have proof that it did in case any dispute arises. Many eBay merchants find that the extra half dollar is a small price to pay for this peace of mind, and it can easily be absorbed into your pricing structure. If you are an online postal customer, you can get online delivery confirmation at no extra charge, which makes your job much easier.

Phishing Attacks

Phishing is a type of social engineering, a type of modern variation on the old "man with a clipboard" attack. In that old swindle, a man with an official-looking clipboard and maybe either a suit and tie or a pair of overalls (depending on how he is trying to disguise himself), walks into your front office, showing what appears to be a work order. The receptionist, of course, thinks that he is legitimate and lets him pass. The con man then proceeds to rifle through the entire office, sometimes even rolling out computers and other valuable hardware on a cart, right in front of everyone.

Phishing does the same thing in an online environment. The attacker attempts to disguise himself as someone he is not and steal your money. This type of attack is especially dangerous for active eBay merchants.

A common attack is to create an e-mail that looks as though it comes from PayPal. The attacker will even use the PayPal logo and even put a phony "warning" against phishing scams at the bottom to make himself look even more legitimate. The e-mail asks you to log into your account and verify your account number by clicking on a link in the e-mail. Instead of going to the PayPal site, you are taken to a site that looks exactly like a PayPal page but is in reality a page run by an attacker. When you enter in your account number, the attacker records it and cleans out your account.

There is technology that can prevent other kinds of attacks, such as viruses and trojan programs, but the nature of these attacks makes it difficult to stop with technology alone. The simplest prevention is never to click on a link inside an e-mail. If you receive an e-mail like this, and if you are selling on eBay, report it to PayPal. If there is any question about any sort of link within an e-mail, do not click on the link. Instead, open up your Web browser and type in the URL directly.

Unscrupulous Buyers

A big part of success is delivering excellent customer service, and that means treating your customers with respect, even though there are some customers who will not treat you with respect and some who will try to defraud you. It is important to be able to tell the difference between a legitimate customer and someone who just wants a free ride. The trick is to be able to do this while not alienating your good customers at the same time.

Some customers will try bidding tricks such as shielding. In this technique, a bidder uses a shill or a partner to drive up the price of the item. This causes other people to drop out of the bidding. At the last minute, the shill also drops out of the bidding, and so the tricky customer can come in at the last minute with a lowball bid and win the auction.

Another trick is for a buyer to win an item, claim they never received the merchandise and reverse payments. It is an online version of shoplifting.

When you are running a physical storefront, it is hard to regulate who walks in the front door, and the same holds true in an online eBay store. Your only protection is to keep track of such bad buyers, block them from future auctions, and avoid selling to buyers with bad feedback ratings.

Hijacked!

It sometimes happens that an attacker is able to steal your account information, and change your password so you can no longer log into your account. If you find that you cannot log in, you may be a victim of a hijack. If this happens, the hijacker can be using your eBay account freely to perpetrate any number of fraudulent transactions, receiving payments for your goods, or buying goods on your account. Take an immediate look around eBay to see if there are any items or bids under your name that you do not know about and contact eBay immediately.

Fraudulent Escrow Service

An escrow service is an excellent way to conduct a high dollar transaction safely, but a fraudulent escrow company can be a disaster. They often operate in conjunction with some sellers or buyers. A common fraud occurs when a seller offers a high dollar item, and when the buyer wins the auction, the seller insists on executing the transaction through a specific, but unknown, escrow service. The buyer makes the payment to the escrow service, the seller gets the money, and the buyer never gets the product. The scam can work in both directions. Merchants can fall victim to phony escrows as well.

Do not be afraid to use an escrow service for high dollar items, but always do some research on them first. If you cannot find any reference to the escrow company on the Internet, chances are it is a phony operated by a scammer. eBay has a recommended escrow service. Use the recommended one or one that is well known and documented as legitimate.

TIP: SHIPPING SCAM

As an eBay seller you will be sure to fall victim to this scam if you ship internationally and you ship parcel post. Since there is no tracking on this type of shipping, you cannot be certain an overseas buyer has or has not received their product. The scam works that the buyer has received the item, but files a PayPal claim stating the item has not been received and does a chargeback. The result is the buyer gets his product and his money back. That is, if they paid for the item using PayPal. This has happened to me twice so far. But that is to be expected, and there is always an element of risk in any business—and each seller must accept a certain level of loss. It is a small price to pay when doing business on eBay.

-Steven Gardner, Chicshades

Arthur and Margo Lemner

Fortunately, Art and Margo have never been the subject of a buyer scam, although the possibility certainly exists for it to happen. "We have, however, been scammed by sellers who claimed they sent an item or made excuses for the delay of receipt of an item until the claim period for eBay and PayPal had expired. The only protection is to file a claim automatically before the claim period ends, regardless of any e-mailed excuses by the seller. I believe the period is 60 days for eBay and 45 for PayPal. This is a short time if your seller is shipping by surface mail from overseas. eBay can get you a refund for up to $200, but has a $25 processing fee, and if the item cost less than that, there is no refund. If your purchase was made by credit card through PayPal, you may also get your credit company to go to bat for you.

"There is also an Internet Crime Complaint Center **http://www.ic3.gov/** in cases of obvious fraud, such as the seller's not returning your e-mails after the claim period has expired. Another recourse is to leave negative feedback. The catch is that the auctions are kept available on your 'My eBay' page for only 60 days, so if it is too late for a claim, it is too late to leave feedback, **unless** you keep a copy of the e-mails regarding the transaction in your regular e-mail folders, not just on eBay. If you have a copy of the auction number, you can access the auction even after the 60 days have expired."

Security

eBay expert Robert Sachs takes plenty of security precautions in his eBay business, and that means both deploying technology and adhering to a set of best practices for security.

> *"I get a lot of phishing e-mail, which I forward back to eBay and PayPal and then block locally. I do not give out my passwords to anyone, and I seldom click a link contained in an e-mail, regardless of who it claims to be from. My friends think I am paranoid. I think I am just being safe.*
>
> *"I also keep my virus scanner up to date, scanning all incoming e-mail, and use several firewall-type products (one via my ISP, one on my local server, one on each workstation), and regularly scan for spyware and malware. I try to automate as much security as possible, so as not to interfere with my regular business hours."*
>
> **-Robert Sachs, RKS Solutions**

Passwords

Memorized passwords are actually one of the weakest security protections. They can be guessed and sometimes stolen with special computer programs called keystroke loggers, which records every keystroke that is made on a computer. Users often write down passwords to avoid forgetting them. Writing them down on sticky notes and putting them under the keyboard, on the monitor, or in a drawer, makes an easy target for any passerby who wants to nose around for a few minutes in hopes of finding one.

In some high-security environments and even in some online banks, users are offered two-factor authentication, which gives them both a memorized password and a physical hardware token that generates a code number that is good for only one use. The benefit of the second one-time-only password is that even if it is stolen, it is of no use, since it cannot be used again. If your bank makes them available, take advantage of it. Unfortunately, eBay does not have such a program, so you are limited to just the single memorized password.

Recommended Security Guidelines

1. Change your password at least once a month.

2. Never write down your password.

3. Do not use common names or words as passwords.

4. Use a mix of alpha and numeric characters.

5. Use at least eight characters for your password.

Firewall

Besides eBay-specific attacks, realize that you are running an online business, and you are vulnerable to all sorts of attacks just like any other business with an Internet presence. Do not make the mistake of thinking that attackers only break into large corporate networks; they break into small office and home office computers as well.

A firewall is a device that is typically deployed through a separate hardware appliance, although it can also be deployed as a piece of software on the same home computer you use for your business. Either way, it does not have to be expensive.

Of course, there is a great deal of attention given to security and larger businesses, especially with high-profile attacks and recent legislation that requires stricter security to be maintained on the part of larger, publicly-held corporations. However, smaller companies also suffer from the same sorts of attacks and can be victims of viruses, trojan programs, and other sorts of malware. Smaller businesses, however, do not have the same work force as larger companies that usually have dedicated personnel who do nothing but security all day. Chances are you are a one-person shop or have only a few employees so that the idea of having a full-time computer security person is out of the question. Many of the major security companies have both software and hardware firewalls that are especially targeted at the small office/home office (SOHO) marketplace, and they are quite affordable. In addition, in many cases, you can be up and running in a single day.

URL Filtering

URL filtering is a type of computer software that filters out certain categories of URLs so that they cannot be allowed onto the computer. They are commonly used in public schools and libraries, as well as in homes where there are young children. If you are the only one who ever uses the computer and you do not have any kids, you may not think you need URL filtering, but think again. There are more dangers lurking out there than you realize.

Some objectionable sites, such as pornographic sites, gambling sites, or hate sites can pop up unexpectedly when you are doing an innocent search. In addition, even if the site comes onto your monitor for just a few seconds until you hit the "back" button, the damage can still be done.

Besides offering offensive content, these sites can also cause serious damage to your computer and network. Pornographic and gambling sites are notorious for holding spy ware, ad ware, trojan programs, and other types of malware; and in many cases, the malware is presented in the form of "active code." This means that the code is launched automatically as soon as the page is viewed. You do not have to do anything. You do not have to click on any buttons, download anything, or take part in any surveys. All you have to do is allow the page to come onto your computer for a few seconds and the malware will find its way onto your computer all by itself. Academic debates about the value of URL filtering and freedom of speech aside, these sites are dangerous and are best avoided.

URL filtering keeps your computer free of Web sites that are likely to contain this sort of malware. URL filtering packages have evolved significantly since they were first released, and they are highly accurate. The much-heralded "false positive" almost never occurs, but if it does, a good URL filtering package allows for easy overrides as needed.

Spyware

Spyware is another category that you must watch out for. It drains your computer resources, affects productivity, and can even steal information directly out of your computer. It is not always even obvious that you have spyware, and it often comes in the form of a trojan program, embedded in some sort of cool freeware you download. Free games, screensavers, and the like often contain spy ware. These little attractive nuisances usually require you to click on some sort of user agreement to get the cool freeware, but that agreement's fine print gives the company the right to embed spyware into your computer.

Sometimes it also comes in through peer-to-peer or instant messaging programs. That is how they make money by giving away something for free. Spyware will watch your Web surfing habits and report them back to a server, which then serves ads and popups to your computer. In the worst case scenario, it is more deadly and may even be used to record keystrokes or steal passwords. A surprising two-thirds of all computers have some type of spyware on them.

There are several inexpensive and free spyware utilities that use a search and destroy method of finding spy ware on your computer and eliminating it. They do have some value, although at that point, the spyware has already found its way onto your system and may have already done as much damage as it can do. Use these search and destroy utilities along with other integrated solutions that spot spy ware as it is trying to enter your computer and get to it before it has a chance to harm your productivity.

Integration

There are several different types of security tools that you will want: anti-virus software, anti-spyware, anti-SPAM, firewall, URL filtering, and if you have more than one location, a secure authentication solution.

It sounds overly much. Buying a separate piece of software, each with a separate interface and separate login, would probably be more than you want to handle. Security companies are moving more toward integrated offerings, however, making your security much easier. This type of integration goes by different names, such as "Unified Threat Management," but what it means is that all of those types of security tools get managed under one umbrella. You get one login, one interface, and can manage everything from one location, and you do not have to be a computer wizard to do it.

In fact, recent research notes that the "scattergun approach" of multiple, separate security products is simply outdated and inefficient and leaves open dangerous security holes that can be exploited easily. This fragmented approach is difficult to manage and is prone to error, simply because there are so many different interfaces, logins, and passwords. The possibility of introducing human error into your security environment is a very real threat. In fact, a misconfigured security system is worse than none at all, since it leaves you with a false sense of security.

Keep It Up To Date

Bad people put out viruses, trojan programs, and other little nasties every day. Keep your anti-virus software up to date with the latest definition files, or you risk letting a dangerous virus through to your network. Some anti-virus packages even include technology that can detect unknown threats that are not even on the list by detecting specific patterns.

Threats From Within

Much of the common thought about information security is to keep out bad guys. The risk of your computer's being infiltrated by someone halfway across the world is very real. Your identity could be stolen by someone in Russia or anywhere else if they use the right tools and a little patience. Fortunately, the technology exists to help you keep these people at bay.

The other threat that we do not consider often is the internal threat. Larger corporations take extra precautions to make sure that they are also protected from internal threats. In fact, some of the attacks that are made on corporate networks are made from within the company itself.

Sure, you do not have a big company. So why worry, right? Think again. Maybe you have one or two part-time employees who use your computer. Maybe you do not even have any employees, but you allow your family to use your business computer. Now surely, your children are not going to try to bring harm to your business, right? That is true, but in many cases, it can be done unintentionally.

Many times, a back door can be opened up unintentionally, and malware let in, even without knowing it. Your kids may be using your computer to run peer-to-peer programs and download music when you are not around. It seems harmless enough, but it is not. Peer-to-peer programs are full of viruses, ad ware, and spyware. When children are downloading the latest hit to their iPod, they may also be downloading a virus into your computer, even though they are blissfully unaware of it and would never do such a thing on purpose.

That is why you protect your computer from internal threats first by deploying a URL filter to keep others away from potentially dangerous sites and also educate your children, employees, spouses, and others as to proper operating procedures and best practices. Teach them never to click on an e-mail attachment unless they are absolutely sure it is from a trusted source, to keep careful track of their own passwords, and to recognize dangerous Web sites.

Get Positive Feedback

The feedback system is a wonderful way of keeping track of who is naughty and who is nice. It is the same concept as word-of-mouth referrals, only it is online. When you run a physical store, your customers may tell their friends they had a good experience or found a great bargain. On the other hand, they may tell their friends about the surly cashier and the product that fell apart when they got it home. The eBay feedback system goes beyond the word-of-mouth concept because it is in writing and lasts forever. As such, it can be a bit unforgiving, but it works. But because it is a written record that is there for all to see, it is vitally important to maintain your positive feedback. A few negative feedback entries will kill an eBay business very quickly.

It is a simple system. You get a point for positive comments, and get a point deducted for negative ones. Both buyers and sellers have feedback ratings. If you encounter a seller who has a low feedback rating and has negative feedback listings, do not sell to that individual. You have a high risk of being a victim of fraud.

At the same time, be very careful about what others say about you. The only way to get a good feedback rating is to treat your customers well and sell them quality products at reasonable prices.

FEEDBACK RATINGS

Currently, I'm proud of the fact that I have a feedback rating of 100 percent, and I work hard to keep that percentage. As with most sellers, I wait until I receive positive feedback before I leave it because then I know the transaction was successful and the buyer is pleased. I feel a buyer should never leave negative feedback unless there is no communication to them via the seller. Most all negative feedback could be avoided if both the buyer and seller were to just communicate, and find a way for both of them to be satisfied.

-Steven Gardner, Chicshades

You Did Not Deserve It

There are buyers out there with a chip on their shoulder. These are the same people who blow their car horns when you are two seconds late starting out from a traffic light and hunt you down in the grocery store if they feel you took their parking spot. They like to yell at waiters in restaurants, and when they encounter an unhappy screaming child in a public place, are quick to point their fingers at the parents and chastise them (even though said individuals have no children of their own). If they do not smoke, they will grab your cigarette out of your mouth and stomp on it. If they do smoke, they will blow it in your face. In short, we are talking about annoying people. There will be occasions when people will abuse the feedback system. They are quick to hold a grudge and will not let you go. Although sometimes negative feedback is indeed deserved, sometimes it is not.

So what do you do? Unfortunately, it is the price we pay for the feedback system. For the most part, the feedback system works very well and serves to protect consumers as well as merchants from unscrupulous people. However, if somebody does make an unfair remark about you or your services in your feedback, you can ask eBay for help, and there is an official Feedback Abuse policy that you can rely on to get undeserved negative feedback removed.

If you do receive a negative feedback, your first instinct may be one of revenge. Instead of leaving the buyer negative feedback as well and having it escalate into a feedback war, contact the buyer and apply some good customer service skills. Ask them how they feel they were not well served and what you could do to rectify the situation or fix the problem for them.

Also, remember that you can reply to feedback comments. If a customer leaves a negative feedback, always log in and create a short reply to the negative comment. In your response, be kind. Leaving a response that insults the buyer will only make you look bad.

Also be aware that for the most part, once you have left the feedback and hit that "Enter" key, you cannot take it back. So be careful. Review what you have written because it is there forever. If you have an unhappy customer, five or ten years from now, their negative comments are still going to be with you. Feedback can be removed, although it is not an easy process under a few special circumstances. eBay has a "mutual withdrawal" procedure, but you must get the cooperation of the person who left the negative mark in the first place, which is not always easy. A negative feedback may also be removed through the SquareTrade mediation process.

Finally, remember that a negative feedback does not have to mean disaster. Lots of negative feedback is a disaster, but one negative and 99 positives still gives you a 99 percent rating, and that is not bad.

Take Full Advantage of Feedback

Your customers have an opportunity to give you a positive rating, and they can also include a few kind words in their review, and they often do. (On the other hand, if you disservice them, be prepared to get blasted!) Those little comments, like "great products, always delivered right away," or "friendly and always answers my questions" are more important than one might think.

Besides having the benefit of those little comments in your feedback section, you can also take further advantage of them in your promotion. Within your listings, on the front page of your store, or in any other advertisements you may have, you can also include a few of these nice little testimonials to help draw more customers to your store.

If you do not have much feedback yet, do not be afraid to ask for it. In addition, if you have a customer you know is happy, another tactic is to approach them with a brief questionnaire and ask them if they would not mind helping you out by answering a few questions. Keep it short and general, with questions such as:

1.   What attracted you to my store?

2.   Did you find our customer service policies helpful?

3.   Was the product you purchased of high quality?

Customer Service

There are advertising tricks you can and should use when creating your store and building up your clientele, but there is still nothing better than good customer service. Running a good shop, delivering good products on a timely basis, answering all questions, not overcharging for shipping, and just treating your customer the way you would like to be treated if you were on the buying end will create happy customers. And happy customers do two things for you: they come back to buy more, and they tell their friends. For a longer discussion of customer service, have a look ahead into Chapter 21. Or you can read my other book, *Superior Customer Service. How to Keep Customers Racing Back to Your Business –Time Tested Examples from Leading Companies* (Atlantic Publishing).

TIP: POSITIVE FEEDBACK

Feedback is always important for both buyer and seller, but there are no "tricks" to getting good feedback, Margo said. "You get positive feedback the hard way: you have to earn it, one sale at a time. Also, buyers tend not to bother leaving feedback, so it is a good idea to inform them that you will not leave positive feedback for them until you have received positive feedback to be certain that they have received their items and that there is no problem with them. Many sellers do not offer refunds unless there is a major problem with the item that was overlooked by the seller—if it is 'not as represented.' This is because most of their prices are already a bargain, and they are giving a great deal of service for the price."

-Arthur and Margo Lemner

TIP: FEEDBACK MANAGEMENT

RKS Solutions has a routine for getting positive feedback. "To help avoid negative feedback, I encourage my buyers to e-mail me in a number of places—starting with the eBay listing and carrying through each e-mail contact with them after that. If there is an issue, I want to know about it **before** *they feel a negative feedback has been earned.*

"With Blackthorne Pro, I never have to worry about forgetting to leave feedback. The easier it is to do something, the more likely it is that it will get done. BTPro makes feedback management easier to manage, and so I am more on top of it and more aware of what needs to be taken care of. Buyers seem to be more willing to leave feedback for me when they can easily see that I leave feedback for my buyers as well."

-Robert Sachs, RKS Solutions

Leave Good Feedback to Get It

We sometimes get lost in the business end of eBay: selling goods, putting them online, and shipping them out. But if you want to get your customers to give you good feedback, you can prime the pump by giving them some, too. Do not forget that sellers can also give buyers feedback ratings and comments. If your buyer paid promptly, leave a good feedback note as soon as you receive payment. They will appreciate it and will be more likely to return the favor and leave you a good feedback as well.

Also, you can send a subtle reminder for your customer to leave feedback. When you send out your goods, include a brief thank you note in the package, and in the text of that note give them a suggestion. Include a line that says something to the effect of, "If you are happy with your product, please take a moment to leave a positive feedback." You can even appeal to them on another level and explain that you are a novice to all this and are still building your business with a comment such as, "As a relatively new eBay merchant, I am going the extra mile to try to ensure that all my customers are happy ones. But I have not been in business long enough to build up a large feedback rating, so please help me succeed in my business by leaving some feedback.

Art and Margo Lemner

To avoid receiving negative feedback, many sellers put information on their auctions or their follow-up e-mails after the sale that tells the buyer to contact them to resolve any problems before leaving feedback. That is eBay's preferred method of resolving conflicts, as misunderstandings can easily arise. Sometimes a buyer will make mistaken assumptions about an auction item based on too little information. Therefore, it is a good idea for sellers to be as complete as possible in describing their items. Also, buyers need to ask any possible questions they can think of before bidding.

If the person you are dealing with is not reasonable, you may receive negative feedback through no fault of your own. Also, if you have to leave negative feedback because the other party is not being honest, they may retaliate with negative feedback. If your feedback rating is high enough, a few negatives will not have a great impact, and it is important to warn others about the problem eBay user. Therefore, I will not hesitate to leave negative feedback if it is deserved. There is a process by which you can add your own short comment in response to a negative feedback, giving you a chance to tell your side of the story. Unfortunately, sellers with very high feedback can be rather arrogant and not treat a customer fairly if there is a problem. You can usually tell from the response comments they make on a negative feedback that they have a major attitude problem.

CHAPTER 11

Cross-Sell and Up-Sell

Why sell one item when you can sell two just as easily? Cross-selling and up-selling are the fine arts of convincing your customers to spend more than they originally intended.

Your best customer is always going to be an existing one. It is easier to make a sale to somebody who has already bought something from you or is in the process of buying something from you, and that is why these two sales techniques are so vitally important. Cross-selling occurs when your customer is buying one item and you then offer them something that complements what they are already buying. Up-selling occurs when your customer is buying one item and you offer them an opportunity to upgrade to a higher quality item of the same type.

One of the simplest examples of cross-selling occurs when you go into a fast food restaurant and the kid behind the counter says, "Do you want fries with that?" Up-selling is when you walk into the same restaurant, and the kid says, "Do you want to super-size that?" You walk away with the extra-huge size soft drink and a vat of French fries, and you leave a little bit more money behind than you had intended.

It is a little different using these techniques online, but it can be done. There are two times when you can engage in these practices: before the sale and after the sale. The most successful eBay vendors and the most successful vendors in general will always use these techniques.

Why Cross-Sell?

Why pay so much attention to the cross-sell? Simply put, it makes you more money. The environment of retail, especially online retail, is very competitive, and customers do not tend to be loyal to individual retailers. The very nature of eBay and of Internet commerce is to allow shoppers to compare prices and products from different vendors. When most shoppers go to eBay, they do not go immediately to a certain eBay store. Rather, they go to the eBay search engine and input the name of the product they are looking for and probably get a list of several dozen eBay stores. This technology makes things easier for shoppers to find the best product at the best price, but it discourages customer loyalty. However, you can mitigate that loss of loyalty with several techniques, including cross-selling and up-selling.

After they have made a purchase, follow-up e-mails and newsletters will drive some return business, but you will get most of those extra sales in the immediate cross-sell at the time of sale. Get them when they are in shopping mode. They have already decided to buy one item. Therefore, offer them something that goes with it right away. Your chances of selling two items in the same sale are actually greater than your chances of selling two items in two separate transactions.

Market research will also show that new customer acquisition is a time-consuming and often costly process, and that is why it is important to maximize the revenue to gain from each sale. You see this in every industry. In the telecom industry, for example, carriers have recently started offering "bundles" of products to maximize the ARPU (average revenue per user). Instead of selling phone service, you can now buy a "triple play" bundle of phone service, Internet service, and cable television service, all at once. You may not be a big telecom company, but you can apply this same philosophy to whatever sort of business you are operating.

Getting Ready for the Cross-Sell

A big part of the cross-sell opportunity takes place before you even list the item. It takes place when you are acquiring your goods to sell. I will go into product acquisition strategies a little more in Chapter 16.

When you are searching out products, whether it is at yard sales, auctions, estate sales, or from wholesalers, finding the perfect product is only half the battle. Once you have found that great buy, that spectacular item you are sure will sell immediately at a high profit, start looking around for other things to go with it. You will always have better luck when you are selling several items in the same category, as opposed to just a random collection of "stuff."

Before the Sale

Before you make the sale, prepare your auction site for possible cross-sell and up-sell by arranging your eBay store the right way. Group your products together in similar categories, so that people will see the possibilities while they are browsing. There are two parts to this type of organization. First, you will create a main page with pictures of several products, and these products will be grouped together with photos of companion products situated adjacent to each other. Second, when the shopper clicks on a given picture, you will have created a separate product page for each item, and when they click on the picture of the main page, they will be taken to this separate product page. On that separate product page, however, you will, of course, include a larger picture of the item with multiple views and a well-written description, but do not stop there. On that separate product page, somewhere near the bottom also include a teaser about companion items. For example, if the product page is about an alligator skin handbag, on the bottom advertise your alligator shoes. Include a smaller picture of the shoes (your cross-sell), with a couple of lines like "What goes great with this beautiful alligator handbag? Matching shoes, of course, and we have them. Click on the picture to find out more."

Post-Sale

After the sale, most eBay guides will tell you the standard protocol, which is to contact the winning bidder, restate the amount of the bid and payment options, ship the product, and ask for positive feedback. That is all fine, but that is not all.

There are automatic e-mailers that will send out automatic e-mail responses to notify bidders of their winning bid, but these automatic e-mails stop short of including an additional sales pitch and really miss the mark. You lose a great marketing opportunity by limiting your follow-up to a simple automated procedural e-mail.

Instead, make your follow-up e-mail a bit more personal. In addition to the necessary information, greet the buyer personally, and include a short and friendly message that tells about other products you have that would go well with what they just bought.

Cross-Sell Outside eBay

If you are really a pro, you are not limiting yourself to eBay. Maybe you have a separate e-commerce site where you sell other goods, or you list on other auctions. Maybe you even have a brick-and-mortar store. Do not hesitate to let your customers know, both in your follow-up e-mail and in subsequent marketing e-mails, where they can find your other offerings.

Packaging

This technique is also an excellent variation of the cross-sell. Packaging simply combines two or more items that go together in the same offering. Do you have a Garfield doll and a Garfield coffee mug? Instead of selling them separately, combine them into a single auction offering. The customer will see it as an attractive combination and a way to get two items at a bargain price. You can offer them at a slightly lower price than you would otherwise because you are selling them both at once and saving on your listing fees and shipping costs.

Selling combinations of items together is a great technique. It takes a little extra work, because you have to find perfect combinations, but the result is that each sale will yield a greater amount.

Accessories

Needless to say, accessories are a great business. If you sell computers, for example, there are many accessories that go with the computer, and you should avail yourself of a large and varied supply. If you want to sell used computers, you should also sell used printers, scanners, mice, glare screens, mousepads, computer books, and other types of peripherals.

There are two approaches that you can take with accessories, and both work well. You can sell all of the accessories separately, but make sure that they are readily accessible and visible from the main page. Do not hide them two or three levels deep. When a shopper clicks on that picture of your used PC, make sure the product page also has information and links to the various accessories they may want or need. Alternately, you can combine the main product with two or three commonly used accessories for a larger primary sale.

Consumables

An ideal cross-promotion is the consumable companion product. If you sell inkjet printers, you know ahead of time that your customer is also going to need to buy ink cartridges. Therefore, you will naturally want to sell ink cartridges as well and perhaps even offer them as a bundle.

In addition to the immediate cross-sell of the consumable companion item, you can have a follow-up cross-sell as well. Keep track of your customers' consumables usage. If they purchased a printer with two ink cartridges, follow up with an e-mail a couple of weeks later when they are likely to be running out. Remind them that you have discount ink cartridges available and direct them to the relevant page on your eBay store.

Collect Customer Data

The cross-sell does not end after the sale. Even if the customer buys a cross-promoted item, you still have an opportunity to sell more in subsequent follow-ups. While you do not want to SPAM people, an occasional marketing e-mail or newsletter (perhaps one a month) is perfectly reasonable. Keep track of all your customers, their e-mail addresses, and their purchase history in a database, and customize follow-up e-mails so that you can periodically offer them products that you know they are likely to be interested in.

Setting Up eBay Cross-Promotions

Fortunately for you, you do not have to do all the cross-selling manually. eBay has a tool for you. You have no doubt noticed that when you view an item for sale, there is usually a small strip at the bottom of the page with a caption that reads something like, "See more great items from this seller." The strip then includes pictures of other items with links to those items.

This automatic cross-promote can be useful or completely useless, depending on how you approach it. If you just let the eBay tool randomly select the other items to view, chances are you will not get a high degree of cross-sell. If you are featuring a purse, and the four cross-promoting items that appear on the bottom of the handbag feature page are a power drill, screwdriver set, hunting cap and a moustache trimmer, you probably are not going to get many clicks on those items.

You have to turn on this option in your "My eBay Preferences" page. Go to that page, click on "Participate in eBay Merchandising," and select "Cross Promote My Items." There are several different options that you can choose from. For example, you may decide to show items by when auctions end, showing the items for which bidding ends soonest. You can show the highest-priced items or just show "Buy It Now" items.

The eBay dialogue will then give you several options to design your cross promotion, and you can choose from several defaults. If all of your items are very similar and in the same general category, you can simply choose to "Show Any Item," and eBay will just rotate items at random in the cross-promote section. In the first dialogue, you will select "Selling Format," "Gallery Items," and "Show My Items Sorted By." Then, you can select what products will show up with individual items if you choose to do so.

However, if you are like many eBay sellers, you have items from several different categories, and you will have some products that just naturally go together. If you sell a coffee grinder, feature the gourmet coffee bean package in your cross-promotion strip.

Custom Shipping for Cross-Sold Multiples

When your buyer buys multiple items, they are going to expect a price break on shipping, since you are going to be shipping multiple items in the same box to the same location. Fortunately again, eBay makes this easy for you. You can automate the process of applying shipping discounts for multiple items to the same buyer. The easiest way to do this is just to plug in a cost for each additional item when you get to the shipping section of the "Sell Your Item" form. A more complicated but probably more accurate method is to use the shipping calculator, which factors in the weight of each item, although this assumes that you want to take the time and trouble to weigh each item before listing it.

TIP: TRACK THE DELIVERY OF YOUR ITEM

eBay sellers do not just sell the item. They have to package it well to avoid breakage, have the item shipped, and often track the delivery. Many inform the buyer of the status of their order, such as when it has been shipped. All that time and expense is wasted if the buyer gets a refund. Many buyers get caught up in a bidding war on an item without considering whether they really want to pay that much. Or they find it too easy to spend too much on eBay, and realize too late that they overspent their budgets.

-Arthur and Margo Lemner

Photography

When you have a brick and mortar store, you will notice that customers love to pick up your goods and handle them before they buy. That is why it is so essential to have excellent photographs of your goods, along with an accurate description. Good photography can make a huge difference in your success on eBay. Therefore, do not shortchange the picture-taking step.

You are going to need two things: a digital camera and image editing software. The digital camera is a necessity in this business. You can take pictures with a conventional film camera, but it is going to be more time-consuming and expensive. Not only will you have to pay for developing costs, you will also have to scan each photograph to digitize it before you can post it on your listing. Arguments about picture quality aside, a film camera is just not practical for an eBay store. The editing software will also be necessary, although it does not have to be high-end. Some of your digital pictures may come out a bit dark, and this software will allow you to adjust the lighting manually. Some of these software packages even have automatic touch-up buttons, where you can just click and have your picture adjusted to the best parameters. The digital software will also allow you to crop the picture, something that you will also find necessary. You may take a photo of an item and find that there is empty space around it, and that is going to make your product less visible once you have posted it. Try to fill up as much of the picture as possible with the item and keep empty space to a minimum.

Choose your digital camera carefully and consider what type of products you are going to be selling. If you are going to be selling small items, like earrings, you may run into some trouble. It is sometimes difficult to get a good close-up shot of a small item with a digital camera without having it come out blurry. If you are only selling larger items, a camera with a lower megapixel rating may be adequate. You can find a three-megapixel camera, for example, for well under $100. But if you are going to focus on smaller items, you will need one of the more expensive, higher megapixel types. Six to eight megapixel cameras can go for over $1,000, but they take superior pictures.

Most digital cameras come with a "digital zoom" option, which is marginally useful in some circumstances but very limited. This digital zoom is not the same thing as a close-up lens attachment. The digital zoom simply enlarges the picture using software interpolation. The result is that you do get a bigger image, but it is going to be fuzzy in many circumstances.

Your Photographic Toolbox

Besides the camera itself, you will need a few other things as well:

Props: Depending on what you are selling, you may want to take pictures with props. If you are selling jewelry for example, you may need to get jewelry displays. A necklace will look better hanging on a black velvet display than it would just laid flat. Fortunately, things like this are inexpensive and can be found at most jewelry supply stores and wholesale shops. You will also want basic props like large sheets of plain cloth, both black and white, to make adequate backgrounds. Background props should be kept to a minimum, so as not to detract from the product itself.

Software: As mentioned above, a good software program for editing your photos is definitely in order. Chances are, your digital camera even comes with a basic image editing package that will probably be more than adequate for basic needs. On the high end, packages like Adobe Photoshop will give you endless editing options, but it is costly and probably unnecessary. Your main concern in image editing is adjusting lighting, focus, and sharpness, and you can do this with any low-end, inexpensive image editing software package. The features available in Photoshop are amazing, but you will not use them for taking eBay pictures.

Fixed tripod: Not everybody has a steady hand, and even if you do, you will find your fixed tripod to be a wonderful time-saver. It is just a simple device that holds your camera steady while you take the picture, but it is very useful in helping you set the camera at precisely the right distance.

Special lenses: You may want to obtain special lenses, like close-up lenses, if your digital camera allows for this option. The less-expensive cameras will not allow for these types of additions, but the higher-end cameras will. Less-expensive, low megapixel digital cameras may well have a digital close-up feature, which may work well in some circumstances, but it will not work as well as a fully-functioning close-up lens.

Lighting: Experiment with lighting. You will not need to buy a whole set of specialty photographic lights, but after taking a few photos, you will quickly see how your background lighting affects your pictures. One or two separate lights that you can stand near your product will do wonders.

Scanner: Although with your digital camera, you will not make heavy use of this, it is still handy to have for those rare occasions when you have a print photograph of a product you want to show. As an added bonus, most scanners also come with image editing software.

Mannequins and clothing stands: If you are selling clothing, the best pictures will show the item in three dimensions. Laying the item of clothing flat will not result in a good picture. Invest in a mannequin or clothing dummy to display the clothing optimally.

Photographic Background

Take a moment to look through eBay and notice the picture quality that you see. You do not have to be a professional photographer, but you can take time to take good pictures. Surprisingly, many people do not do this. The background, for example, is a simple concept that is not expensive, but it can make a big difference in picture quality. Taking a picture of a ladies' handbag sitting on your kitchen table is unprofessional. It is completely unforgivable if the picture shows your leftovers from lunch.

That is not to say you cannot use your kitchen table. Most amateur photographers taking eBay pictures do. But take an extra step to make sure that it does not look like a kitchen table. It is easy to do. Get two or three large pieces of cloth, one black, one white, and maybe one or two other basic, plain colors. Do not ever use patterns. Cover your table with it. If your product is dark colored, use the white background; if the product is light, use the dark background.

You will use the cloth in two dimensions, to cover the flat area, and to cover the vertical space behind your product. Use the same cloth to create a standing platform, so you do not get your windows or walls in the picture. In some cases, just something simple and ordinary, like a book, can be propped on end and the cloth draped over it.

How Many Pictures to Take?

For some basic, commodity items, you do not need multiple shots. If you are selling ink cartridges for computer printers, your customer does not really care about what it looks like from the side, just so long as it is the right model and color. One picture is sufficient in this case.

However, for items such as clothing, antiques, or collectibles, a simple front-on photograph is just not enough. You will need several pictures that show the item from different angles.

eBay Picture Gallery Features

You may wish to use the eBay Picture Gallery features, especially if you have a high-quality item. Use these features carefully though, since you will pay by the image. These special features will let you, for example, super size photos, so a shopper can click on a thumbnail of it to link to a larger picture.

If you want to have multiple pictures to show your product from different angles, eBay's "slideshow" format is very useful, and makes for a very attractive listing. Again, you must pay for each image, so a slideshow with multiple images can get costly, and for low-priced items they may not make much sense. Once you have uploaded your pictures, just select the "picture show" option, which will transform your pictures into a slideshow. The picture show option itself is free, although you do pay for each image being hosted. Some third-party image hosting services will also offer you a slideshow option.

Where to Park Your Photos

Your photos have to be hosted somewhere. eBay Picture Services is the primary method for storing and uploading photographs, and if you only have a few items on auction, this is by far the most practical. For larger users, Picture Services also offers a subscription rate. With a subscription, you can upload pictures in bulk, add up to 12 pictures for each listing, and store them on eBay indefinitely. It is costly though, and there are other services that you can use to save money. Alternately, if you are able to run your own Web server (you need a static IP address), you can store them on your own computer.

Remember that although your first photo on an eBay listing is free, eBay charges for all subsequent images. It can get costly. Using a third-party image hosting service can save you money if you have a high volume of products.

Pictures in Your E-Mail

When you send your follow-up e-mails, newsletters, and other marketing material, you will also want to take advantage of your photographic skills. If you are sending a follow-up e-mail for example, to let your existing customers know you have some new products, do not limit that e-mail to plain text. At one time, when everybody had slow dial-up connections, you were limited and graphics were never welcome, but that is no longer the case.

Of course, do not overdo it. An e-mail with a dozen photographs in it will still take up too much space in sometimes limited e-mail boxes and will take a long time to download.

However, describing a new product and including a couple of small thumbnails in an attractive display will increase your business and will make your e-mail message stand out.

Copyrighting Your Photographs

Sometimes eBay sellers may attempt to take the lazy man's way out, and instead of taking their own pictures, look through eBay to find somebody else selling the same thing and steal their picture. Naturally, eBay frowns on the practice, but it is surprisingly common. Some eBay merchants take the extra step of copyrighting their photographs by placing a text line within the image. You can do this with your image-editing program. Just add a single line that shows your eBay user ID number, and a copyright symbol. If you have done this, and somebody else uses your photograph, you can report the guilty party to eBay.

Is it necessary to copyright your picture and add the text line? It depends on your pictures. If you are the person selling inkjet cartridges, and you have spent 15 seconds taking a picture of an inkjet cartridge, it does not really matter. It is a commodity item and it looks pretty much the same, no matter who takes the picture. On the other hand, you may spend time setting up a photograph of a specialty item, and you want to use your photographic skills to give yourself an edge over the competition. In such a case, you surely do not want other people to lift your photograph.

Common Photography Mistakes

Even the best of us takes a dud photograph every now and then. Keep in mind that taking close-up photographs of your items for sale is different from taking your vacation shots of the Grand Canyon. It is not quite as simple as point-and-shoot. Here are a few common mistakes eBay vendors make:

- **Cellophane glare**. Items that are pre-packaged in cellophane wrapping are hard to photograph. The light from the flash will inevitably reflect on the cellophane, and you will get a big bright spot right in the middle of your item. There are two ways to avoid this: first, turn the item to an angle and do not take the picture straight on. The second way is simply to remove the wrapping.

- **Distracting background**. As mentioned above, it is best to always use a plain background that contrasts with the color of the item. Do not use that paisley bed sheet as a background drop!

- **Too much white space.** You will often see items that take up only a small space in the photograph listed on eBay. Do not make your item hard to see! Make it take up as much of the photographic space as possible. Fill up your photograph with what you are selling.

CHAPTER 13

Writing Your eBay Text

Your customers cannot pick up your product and examine it before buying, and so the text you attach to it is just as important as a good photograph. If they cannot touch it, all you have is photography and words. In the previous chapter, we looked at the photography. Now we will look at how to describe it.

Words, Words, Words

A poorly written description will make you look unprofessional. If there are mistakes in your description, such as spelling errors or poor grammar, it will reflect badly. Subconsciously, the buyer will see a poor quality description, and will translate that into a poor quality product. "Jewelry" can be beautiful. "Jewlery" is always perceived as substandard and worthless, regardless of how high quality the stones may be and how perfect the setting. "Full carat, near-flawless diamond jewelry" will get you a better bid than will "full caret, near-flawless diamond jewlery."

Again, take a moment to surf through some eBay listings. The number of obvious language errors is shocking. Always proofread each listing, and if possible, have somebody else proofread it as well.

Copywriting is an art form. People study it in college and larger companies hire professionals to create effective catalog text. eBay is a competitive marketplace, and in many cases, there are hundreds of other products that are the same as yours. Your description may be the only way to differentiate what you have from all the rest. Look at the following two descriptions:

1. This is an 18-inch freshwater pearl necklace with a silver clasp. Includes gift box. (See picture.)

2. This beautiful, 18-inch freshwater pearl necklace features an attractive silver, rose-shaped clasp that is easy to open and close. The 6.5 mm pearls are well shaped and near-perfectly round, with a shine and lustre you would expect from only the highest quality pearls. The pearls are cultured and originate from the pearl farms of the Yangtze River area, which are well known for producing some of the world's highest-quality freshwater pearls. Comes in a velvet-lined gift box for your special presentation.

Too often, eBay sellers create descriptions that are functional but not very creative. You must go beyond simply telling your potential customer what you have. You have to make them want it.

Do not expect to place pictures and basic descriptions on eBay and be successful. You have to think like the marketers on Madison Avenue.

Take a minute to pick up a nationally distributed slick magazine and look at the ads. Read the text carefully. Those ads do more than make you aware of a product. They make you want to go out and buy it. Sure, I hear you resisting. "No, those ads do not influence me," you say. There may even be those among you that think advertising and marketing are evil. If you believe that, you need to get out of the eBay business. If you want to succeed, get used to the idea. Selling good products at a fair price just does not cut it. You have to use advertising and marketing techniques to make people want what you have and want to buy it from you, even if the next person has exactly the same thing for a nickel cheaper.

Be Descriptive

Your customer is not able to pick up your product and try it on for size, so you have to be as descriptive as possible. To say that you are selling a "pink cashmere scarf" is not enough. Describe its texture in detail. Tell your customer exactly how big it is (width and length), and describe the shade of pink. There is a world of difference between "hot pink" and "pink pastel." If you are selling a piece of electronics, do not just tell what it is. State the model number and manufacturer and list all the features.

Besides appropriate and descriptive adjectives, you can take your descriptive copy up a notch by not only describing the product, but also describing the use of it so that the potential buyers can visualize themselves enjoying it. Here are a few ideas:

1. **Describe the environment that results from use of the product**. "This pristine coffee grinder will fill your kitchen with the sweet aroma of Arabica and the fragrance of French roast."

2. **Describe how it will "feel" to use the product.** "This pashmina, made from the finest cashmere from the Himalayas, feels so delicate against your skin, you will never want to take it off."

3. **Describe the benefit that will result from using the product.** "This ingenious kitchen wizard will cut your meal preparation time in half."

Tell Them How They Benefit

When you look at those ads in this week's issue of *Time Magazine*, you will notice that in addition to doing a good job of describing whatever product is being advertised, the copywriters will also usually add some verbiage to describe the benefit that will come to the buyer if they go out and immediately purchase their product.

It may seem obvious to you, and many people think it may be unnecessary, but this is a big part of good copywriting. Sure, it is true that if you are selling mouthwash, the benefit is obvious. You can assume that people will know that if it says "mouthwash" on the label, their benefit from buying the product will be sweeter-smelling breath. "My customers are not idiots," I hear you say. "They know what mouthwash does." True enough, but it does not hurt to reinforce the message.

Copywriting creates a perception of quality. All mouthwash gives you better-smelling breath, but if you are selling your own particular brand of mouthwash, you want to create the perception that your breath will smell better with this product than it would with any other. You want to create the perception that after using your mouthwash, their breath will smell so sweet that women will instantly fall at their feet, they will get a great raise and promotion at work, and the IRS will not audit them. These fabulous benefits will not, of course, accrue to the person who buys the other person's mouthwash.

Before you write your listing, stop and consider what possible benefits could accrue to the person who buys your product. Every product you sell has some sort of benefit, and it is up to you to put it into words. It may even be obvious, but you need to put it out there. Here are a few examples:

PRODUCT	BENEFIT
Retro-style '50s dress	You will be ready for the next sock hop
Cashmere pashmina	Texture feels warm and soft
Computer printer	Fast output, crisp letters
Sexy nightgown	You will make his eyes pop out of his head
Ethernet switch	Connect up to four computers
Viagra	Longer-lasting . . . well, you get the idea

Keep It Short

By "keep it short," I do not mean that you should present a bare bones, basic, and functional description. The functional must always be enhanced with a little bit extra. Describing the benefit can be something as simple as, "You'll look stunning with this beautiful pearl necklace," or "Enjoy your mornings a little bit more with our gourmet coffee beans." It does not have to be long, but it does have to create a sense of heightened desire.

However, it is certainly possible to go overboard. Have you ever seen those ads on the Web, peddling some sort of get-rich-quick scheme, book, or set of tutorial videos? It seems to go on and on forever. I have seen some that go well over 3,000 words or about the size of a medium feature article in a magazine. It is far too long for an advertisement and nobody is going to read it all.

While you do have to focus on creating an image and a desire, you must also do so with an economy of words. Use shorter sentences and paragraphs. If there are many details that need to be listed, use charts or bullet points to make it easier to read. In addition, always try to read your description aloud before you have decided to keep it.

Last, and this is the key to every writer's success, do not ever be afraid to throw out what you have written. If it looks too long, or just does not sound right, edit it. Cut some out. Throw it out entirely and start from scratch. Even the best writer realizes that his or her words are not sacred.

KEEP AUCTION LISTING SIMPLE

Art himself is well known around his community as a fine artist; therefore, he has a good eye for display. Nonetheless, they said that the best auction listing is a simple one. "We tried to be as specific as possible in our auction titles, so that the items would come up in a search that a buyer might be doing for those particular items. The titles are limited. We avoided buzzwords like "wow" and "look," since these words are a waste of space. Sometimes it is a good idea to give alternate words for the item or to include singular and plural in case the searches do not include the various possibilities. As far as the listing pages themselves, we also avoid adding 'wallpaper' or anything unnecessarily fancy, because that makes the page load more slowly for the prospective buyer. Buyers are interested in the auction items and not in how interesting the auction page is visually. A better use of time is to provide a good, thorough description and several good photographs of the item if it is a one of a kind or rare collectible. Photos are less important if the item is relatively new and the buyers are very familiar with what it should look like."

-Arthur and Margo Lemner

Keywords

Keep in mind that potential buyers are going to find your products by entering words into eBay's search engine, and you will want to enter in appropriate keywords in both the text and your title. These keywords will help your buyers find your product, so choose them carefully.

Do not limit yourself to one or two keywords. Think about the product for a while and realize that the potential buyer may actually try to search for a product using one of several keywords, and often, they will use keywords that you may not have considered.

Keyword listing is an integral part of the copywriting process. In addition to listing the name of the product itself, use additional keywords that describe it in as many ways as you can think of. Other keywords should describe the material, manufacturer, and model, as well as what country it may have come from. Realize that your buyers may not be good spellers and include keywords that account for variations in spelling.

Writing Your Title

The title in your product description is the first thing your potential buyers will see when they come to your page. You must use it to your advantage. The title is what will convince them to look further to examine the description and picture.

First, resist the temptation to use words like "WOW!" in your title. There are far too many "WOWs" in eBay titles, and it is a completely useless word. It means nothing to people, and it is not convincing. Similarly, you really do not need to add ten exclamation points, and it is very distracting to put everything in all capital letters.

You have the option of also adding a subtitle, and this is often a good strategy, if you can afford the extra 50 cents or so that eBay charges you for it. Your subtitle can enhance your title by offering additional description and should flow nicely into the text description.

Colloquial Tone

You do not have to write your descriptions in the King's English, but if you are going to use a colloquial tone, be careful and use it sparingly. It takes a good writer to carry this off. When creating your listing, on eBay especially, a conversational tone is usually good, but some people attempt to take it a step further by trying to write in a dialect. And in some cases, it works. If you are selling Playstation games, your audience is going to be young people, so it is probably okay to work in a bit of the youth slang into your descriptions. If you are selling kitsch from Appalachia, it may work to say something like, "It's purtier than the parson's wife on a Sunday mornin'."

Use Copywriting Strategies Everywhere

I have given you a few tips on how to write an effective eBay listing here, but your eBay listing represents only part of the writing that you will be doing. Much of your business revolves around the words you create. Those words are the fuel for your business. They will be what makes people decide to spend money in your store rather than somebody else's.

Keep these techniques in mind in every aspect of your business. Besides your eBay listings, you will also want to continue using effective copywriting techniques even in mundane things like your follow-up e-mail. They can be more than a simple e-mail that says, "Congratulations, you have placed the winning bid for a 19th Century Siamese vase." Pay attention to wording in every piece of text you create, no matter how ordinary or routine it may seem. You never stop marketing.

CHAPTER 14

The Power of Text

You can drive traffic to your eBay store by becoming an expert. For example, if you sell fishpond supplies, publish a separate, informational Web site with excellent articles about how to build fish ponds and link to your eBay store from that site. If you gain an online reputation as somebody who is an expert on a subject, you will gain with greater sales. You may have to spend some time answering questions and providing occasional free advice, and you may want to start spending time with online chat rooms and bulletin boards.

While you usually cannot advertise directly on message boards, just being there will provide you with an opportunity to enhance your reputation as somebody who is knowledgeable about your subject matter. What happens when people see you as the man who knows all about Cambodian pottery? When they want to buy a piece, they will ask you where to go. You then direct them to your eBay store.

Informational Web Sites

When people search the Web, sometimes they are looking specifically for a product to buy, but more often than not, they are looking for information about products that they are thinking about buying. It has become common to do a little Internet research on a product or product category before spending money on it.

Another option is to create one or more informational Web sites, separate from your eBay presence. The purpose of the site is an indirect sell. You will not be selling anything directly from this Web site so that you do not have to worry about the mechanics of setting up an e-commerce site. The purpose of this site is information only. Think of it as a big advertisement for your eBay store. The premise behind the informational Web site is to get it listed with all the major search engines, so people will find it when they are seeking information about whatever product category you are dealing in. Once they go to your informational Web site, you provide them with informative articles and information that relate to your product category, and you offer a link to your eBay store. It is not going to work for every category, but this technique works surprisingly well for a large number of product categories. The nice thing about it is that it costs very little to maintain, and once you have set it up, you do not have to do much to maintain it.

The first thing to do is to consider your product category. Have books been written about it? Suppose you sell antiques. There are thousands of books and Web sites about antiques and subcategories of antiques, and people wanting to buy antiques would be fools not to do a little research before spending money on something. They will want to know the approximate value of the type of antique they are interested in, where they come from, and something about the history. And of course, there are always interesting and entertaining stories floating around about somebody who found one for $1 and sold it for $10,000. In short, if you deal in antiques, you could create a wonderfully informative and entertaining content-based Web site around this subject. People wanting information about your particular subcategory of antiques would find it on the search engines, enjoy reading your information, and are very likely to follow your link to your eBay store.

Your informational Web site does not need to be long, ten pages is a good length. Be sure to include the link to your eBay store on every page. It should be well written, informative, and well researched. It may take you a little time to put it together, but you may find it to be worth your time. If you are not an expert on your product, now is the time to become one. Check some books out of the library, do some Web surfing on your own, and pull together all the information you can find. Do not lift anything verbatim, but use the information to come up with your own narratives. If your writing skills are not what they could be, either have somebody edit your work or hire a professional writer to create the entire site for you. If you do not know professional writers, you can find one on eLance **www.elance.com**, an auction site for freelance workers.

After you have the Web site written, the next step is to put it together using a Web site development program. Some office suites come with one installed, or you can purchase one inexpensively. I prefer SiteSpinner, which is inexpensive and easy to use. Be sure to include a header with all of the relevant keywords included.

Once your site is written, designed, and uploaded to your hosting service, you are not done yet. You still have to submit it to the search engines so that people can find it. There are plenty of services out there that will offer to get you listed on the search engines for a fee, but you can do the work yourself for free. It is not hard, and each of the major search engines has clear instructions about how to go about it. The fee-based services may offer to get you listed on "hundreds" of search engines, but do not be tempted. Get listed on Google, Yahoo, and MSN. The rest are too small to make that much of a difference, and they are not worth the expense.

Within your informational Web site, you should also include contact information. Include your e-mail address prominently so that visitors can contact you if they have any questions.

Letter with Your Product

Many eBay sellers miss a good opportunity to promote themselves with their existing customers. When somebody buys a product from your eBay store, and of course, once you are paid, you eagerly and carefully package the product and enclose a receipt. If you are polite, you include a short, "Thank you for your order," on the receipt or on a separate piece of paper. However, you can do more.

Consider that existing customers are your best and most promising source of future business. Take the opportunity to cultivate that relationship a little bit more when you are shipping out an order. Besides the receipt and the brief "Thank you," enclose another separate letter, or better yet, a professionally designed brochure that tells not only about your business, but also more about the product line.

Even if you only want to include a short thank you note, you can embellish it a little to tell your customer more about the product.

Here is an example:

"Thank you for ordering the Benjarong china tea set. I know you will enjoy it. My own guests always are delighted when I bring it out for afternoon tea. The history of Benjarong also makes a fascinating story to tell your guests. This particular style of china originates in Siam. Each piece is hand-painted by a highly trained artisan, using a combination of five colors. That is what "benjarong" means. In the ancient Pali language, it means "five colors." You will notice that one of the colors is always gold, and the gold color on your tea set is real 14 carat gold. At one time, Benjarong china was made exclusively for the royal Siamese court, and commoners used a lesser quality tea set. Today, anybody can buy and enjoy this fine quality china. Please feel free to check back to my eBay store from time to time to see what other fascinating and historical tea sets, china, and vases I find on my travels throughout the Far East."

The above is more interesting than just a short, "Thanks for your order," and is much more likely to result in a return visit.

E-Mail Newsletters

Do not make the mistake of thinking that any e-mail you send out promoting your site is going to be considered "SPAM." E-mails that really are SPAM have caused some people to paint all e-mail communications with a broad brush, but it does not have to be so. In fact, e-mail is a valid form of marketing, and the most successful e-commerce organizations use it often.

SPAM is a type of e-mail advertisement that has very little valuable content, and it is sent out on an unsolicited basis to a very large audience. When a marketer buys a mailing list and sends out a million ads with a link to a site where he sells Viagra, that is SPAM, and the recipient has every right to get indignant about receiving it. But creating a monthly e-mail newsletter to send to your customers and others who may have requested it from your Web site is another thing entirely. Your e-mail newsletter's purpose is to sell products, without a doubt. But it is not just a simple advertisement. The purpose of the e-mail newsletter is to create a sense of closeness between yourself and your customer. You are sending them this newsletter to tell them entertaining stories and to give them informative articles about a subject they are interested in. In so doing, you position yourself as an expert in the field, and the recipients of that newsletter are more likely to come to your eBay store when they do want to buy something.

Like the informational Web site described above, your e-mail newsletter is meant to be informative and content-rich. Its purpose, other than advertising your site, is to give people something of value. And like the informational Web site, your e-mail newsletter should also be well-written and well thought out. You may wish to consider hiring a professional writer to create the content for you.

Your "About Me" Page

Do people really read these? You bet they do. And if you approach it right, it is a great way to build more business. First, the "About Me" page is vitally important, simply because of the natural distrust that people often have in regard to buying online. Nobody wants to buy something from a stranger. Buying online from a nationally recognized vendor does not cause this sort of problem, but how do people know that they will get the same quality of service from Joe's eBay Electronics? The fact is that buyers know that **Sears.com** is a real site with real products, but do they know the same thing about Joe? No, they do not. And that is where this little informational page comes in. The "About Me" page gives your potential customer more information about your company and about you personally. It makes them feel more comfortable about you and eliminates the nervous feeling that they are buying something from an anonymous entity halfway across the country.

Most security experts will advise against ever buying anything online from a company that does not give information like a phone number, e-mail contact, physical location, and maybe even the name of the owner. If your e-commerce site, whether it is eBay or anything else, takes a completely anonymous approach, you will lose business because people will naturally be suspicious.

You can add an "About Me" page on your eBay store for free. It does not have to be long, but take some time to create something that will make your visitors feel at home. Tell them about yourself. Sure, you sell antique farm equipment, but they already know that from looking at your site. On this page, tell about how you grew up on the farm and relate a few funny stories about things that happened to you. Talk about how you personally have found old farm equipment to be fascinating ever since you were a kid and used to play on your grandpa's tractor. In addition, do not be afraid to use your real name, not just "Bob642" from "Bobsantiques." If you can, put a photograph of yourself in there as well and make it relevant. Place a photo of yourself in overalls, holding a pitchfork, and standing next to old milk jugs. Those little additions make your customer feel like they are dealing with a real person.

The eBay Listing

Your eBay listings are more than just descriptions and pictures. They are an artistic presentation that needs to be graphically pleasing. The listings are the foundation of your business. There are as many different strategies for creating listings as there are eBay sellers, but there are a few key things to understand. When you write your listing, you wear the hat of a creative writer, an advertising executive, a public relations professional, and an editor. You are a salesperson, a businessperson, and a schmoozer.

Tell Stories and Wear a Big Hat

Take a weekend trip to the flea market. Notice something? There is always a core group of flea marketers that come back every weekend. They are successful at what they do, and while newcomers often give up after a few weeks, this core group seems to have something that the others do not. Making good money at the flea market is hard. Newbies try it out for a while and decide that it is impossible. Yet, people still do it, and they still make money. How? Because they know how to make a presentation. They know how to make people feel comfortable, and they know how to talk about a product. Flea marketers are the best schmoozers in the world. They are gregarious.

eBay is very much like one very large flea market. People will try their hand and fail, but there is a core group that really knows how to do it. You have to take the element of success from the flea marketers and translate that into the virtual world. You have to tell many stories.

In the world of eBay, what that means is that you have to be descriptive in your listings, add plenty of personal stories and insights, and let your visitors in on a little bit of your personal life in your "About Me" page. Make yourself different. Make your site stand out above the others at every opportunity. You can do this in three ways:

1. Through design

2. Through your product mix

3. Through the prose you create to describe your products.

The mechanics of creating a listing are simple, and you can pick up how to do that easily on eBay. But it is what you do with that listing that makes the difference. Just as in the flea market, anybody can rent a table for the weekend and set out a bunch of stuff with price tags on them. But not everybody can put life into each and every one of those products.

You may also notice that those flea marketers are never afraid to tell something about themselves. They will always tell you their name and often the names of their wives and children, possibly even their ex-wives and high school sweethearts, and anything that has happened to them (real or imagined) if it has something remotely to do with a product that is on their table. They will tell it, no matter how bizarre or embarrassing.

This is what you have to do in the eBay world as well. Instead of just describing an item, describe how you used it to meet your first wife, how you found it while trekking through the Burmese jungle, or how you modified one once to replace a burned-out carburetor in your '62 Studebaker. Every item has a story, even if it is just how much you enjoy using it every day. Find that story, and you will make your sale. From the buyer's point of view, what is better than finding the perfect antique that nobody else has: finding the perfect antique that has a story attached to it. Almost every item in my home has a story behind it, from the bamboo scroll that was presented to my wife in Tibet by a band of wandering Buddhist monks, to the teakwood spirit house that was used in old Siam as a domicile for one's dead ancestors. Now take that bamboo scroll. If I said to you, "I have a bamboo scroll," it may sound moderately interesting, but not very. But when I add the story about how my wife got it when she was in Tibet, you want to see it right away.

> *"Keep your listings easy to read, concise, and focused. Have a solid, enforceable returns policy and stick to it. Make exceptions for your best customers. Whether or not they say so, they are talking about you to their friends and generating more sales."*
>
> **-Robert Sachs, RKS Solutions**

Different Types of Listings

eBay has three basic types of listings, and you will want to pay attention to all three. A beginning eBay seller may want to test the waters with just a few auction listings, but once you have achieved a little success, the greater yields will come in when you experiment with all three types. These three types are the auction listing, the fixed price listing, and the store listing. Each has its relative advantages and using a combination of all three will maximize your opportunities.

Auction listings are the basic listings that allow shoppers to bid on your product. These listings can be found in the eBay search engine, and they are important to drive traffic to your other auctions or to your eBay store. A shopper who does not know about you yet may be searching for an item that you have, and that is how they will find you. Once they have clicked on the item listing in the search results and go to your listing, you have an opportunity to sell them an item and to sell yourself. From your listing, they can go to your eBay store. They can read your prose, and they can learn a little more about you and what you have to offer. That is why the auction listing is an all-important component of your eBay success. It is not only a way to sell products. It is a jumping off point to get your shoppers to explore more of what you are all about. In that respect, even an auction that does not yield a sale or a profit still has some advantage in terms of broader marketing.

Fixed price listings, on the other hand, do not allow for bidding. They allow you to offer something at a fixed price. Depending on what you are selling, this option may make sense. You may have an exceptionally rare item, one that you have put money into, and an auction may not be the best way to sell it. These listings too will turn up in the basic eBay search results, and the fixed price listing can serve the same purpose as the auction listing in terms of broader marketing and driving traffic to the eBay store.

Finally, the last type of listing is the eBay store listing. Here, you sell fixed-price items only (no auction items), although these are separate from individual fixed-price listings. Products in your eBay store, unlike auction and fixed-price individual listings, will not come up in the eBay search results. This is a big difference. When you list products in your eBay store, you have to get customers to find them in other ways. Here is the reason: most people who have eBay stores also keep some items out for auction as well to drive traffic to the store.

TIP: KEEP YOUR LISTING SIMPLE

When creating his listings on eBay, Bob goes for the simple approach. "I try to keep my listings clean and easy to read, use a large primary item image (with links to additional images should the buyer want to see more), and keep my terms as simple and compact as possible. No gyrating graphics, no irritating sound files, no huge graphics that take forever to load – quick, clean, and clear works best for me.

"Blackthorne Pro has an excellent WYSIWYG auction template editor, allowing me to design and develop very professional auction layouts without having to know much HTML at all. It also allows me to edit the HTML code directly when I want to use features the editor does not support. Over the years, I've developed a style, keeping it fresh with semi-annual updates and minor redesigns."

-Robert Sachs, RKS Solutions

The Details

Your listing, besides being written creatively, also has to include some basic details besides the product information. On the listing itself, you should make sure that your shipping policy and rates are clearly stated, as well as things like shipping schedules. Do you send items out within 24 hours of payment confirmation? Then say so in the listing. That is important to know.

SOME OTHER NUTS-AND-BOLTS DETAILS TO INCLUDE IN THE LISTING ARE::

- ❑ Return Policy
- ❑ How to pay (checks, money order, Paypal)
- ❑ Any guarantees you may offer
- ❑ Other details about yourself, such as whether you are a Powerseller or Square Trade member.

Appearance

Besides the content of the listing, how it looks is also important. There are many ways to vary an eBay listing, and it is important to know what you should and should not do.

One thing to avoid is making it too busy or flashy. Avoid unusual highly stylized type fonts in favor of something plain and basic. There is a reason for that, and it is simple. A plain type font is just easier to read for most people. Leave out the Old English and cartoon fonts. Similarly, unusual borders and heavy graphics should be avoided, and under no circumstances should you ever add a music file to a listing. Opening up a Web page that plays music is not fancy or clever. It is just annoying and it makes the page load too slowly.

Experiment with the style of your listings to see what looks best and works well and create a basic template for yourself that you can repeat for all items. Once you find a format that works, stick with it.

Keep It Positive

Almost every eBay seller who has been selling for any length of time has had some negative experiences, and you may be tempted to let those experiences color your perception of eBay and how you do business. Sure, you hate it when you get non-paying bidders or somebody leaves negative feedback that you did not deserve. If you look through the eBay listings and pay attention, you will see sellers with negative messaging in their listings, designed to try to avoid a repeat of these negative experiences.

Here is the scoop on that: you are in business, and you will have some negative experiences. End of story. Get used to it. It is part of the package, and you are not going to avoid it. Writing listings with negative statements creates an atmosphere of intimidation and unfriendliness. Regardless of how many people have wronged you on eBay, you still have to treat your customers with respect.

Do you like it when you go into a store and the store detective follows you around? Or when you go to the warehouse store and after you have already paid, a clerk at the door checks through your cart to make sure you are not walking out with something you did not pay for? It is creating an atmosphere of suspicion and distrust. Customers do not like to feel that they are being suspected of a crime, and it makes them not want to go back. When you walk into the store, you want to feel like a guest and be made to feel welcome. The same holds true in your eBay business.

There is an undue amount of whining within eBay's listings. Do not clutter your listings with complaints about people who do not pay or do not understand your terms. Make your visitors feel welcome, and regardless of how many bad experiences you have had in the past, avoid statements like the following:

STATEMENTS TO AVOID IN YOUR LISTINGS
• "Please read the entire listing before bidding!" (Problems Assumes buyer is an idiot.)
• "I have to send e-mails sometimes three or four times before getting a response from buyers. Please respond immediately!" (Problem Whining.)
• "I will cancel your bid if I see that you have a lot of negative feedback." (Problem: Probably a good idea in practice, but you do not have to say it on your listing.)
• "Do not bid if you do not plan to pay!" (Problem: Assumes the buyer is a flake.)
• "If payment is not received in three days, negative feedback will be given!" (Problem: Threatening your customer.)

Yes, it is true, some of your shoppers are idiots, but always give them the benefit of the doubt until they prove themselves otherwise.

Finding Products

There are thousands of places, online and otherwise, where you can buy nice wholesale goods. The problem there is that everybody else on eBay has already bought goods from those places and you will have nothing with which to differentiate yourself. eBay does not work well for people who sell commodity items. You need to find something more unusual that nobody else has.

Your eBay business is not about selling things on eBay. Not really. Selling is just a small part of it; the fun really begins before you have created the listing and you are out trying to find the products to list. Sourcing your goods is what will make or break you. A bad product, no matter how well designed and well worded your listing, is not going to make you any money. Your product mix, the quality, and the scarcity of what you acquire are going to determine your sell-through level.

Some people who start out on eBay make the unfortunate mistake of believing that they will sell everything they list. Regrettably, it does not usually happen that way. But there is a level of acceptable loss, and you will have to determine that on your own. You will have to figure in your acquisition costs, your eBay expenses, and your time involved. You will have to determine what percentage of products you will have to sell to turn a profit. You may, for example, be acquiring goods at very low cost and be able to turn a good profit if you are only selling half of what you are listing. In addition, as for the other half, well, you will have a ready supply of Christmas and birthday presents.

The Product Mix

Besides where to find the products, you must also consider what products you want to find. If you can specialize in a few areas, you are more likely to become successful because you will become knowledgeable about those areas and get to know the collectors. Nevertheless, you must also be cautious and avoid stagnation. eBay is a highly fluid market, and what sells well one month may not sell very well the next. Do not get too attached to any one category and do not be afraid to branch out.

Think beyond the ordinary. There is money to be made in selling day-to-day products, but it is a little different on eBay than it is anywhere else. If you do insist on trading in ordinary commodity goods, you have to realize that you are selling something that eBay shoppers can probably get at a store within a few miles of their home and you have to give them some incentive to buy it from you instead. The incentive is usually price. Take those portable fluorescent light bulbs that people have started using to replace their regular bulbs. They are energy efficient and great, but you can also get them at any corner drugstore, usually for about $2 each. If you can somehow lay your hands on a shipment of them that has been deeply discounted, and you can sell them for $1 apiece, you will make money. However, if you list them on eBay for the same price they can get them at the neighborhood Safeway, you are out of luck.

Packaging and Bundling

You can make your products seem like a better deal sometimes if you package products together that complement one another. The idea here is to take two or more products, and instead of selling them in separate auctions, sell them as a set. You will increase your odds of selling both products in one sale, as opposed to selling only one!

Retailers do this all the time. Look at the computer advertisements. When you buy a computer, many times you do not just buy the computer. They sell a bundle that includes the computer, an inkjet printer, some software, and other assorted odd peripherals. The result is that you get more money from each customer, you have better odds of selling all the products, and you save on your eBay listing fees.

Consumable Goods

Goods that get used up and have to be purchased again periodically are also a good sort of item to sell. If you are offering a good deal, you can get repeat business using this approach. Take something like inkjet cartridges. This market is highly competitive, and buyers are always looking for a deal. Granted, it is a commodity item, and they can be found anywhere. From that perspective, it is a bit of a hard sell on eBay, but if you can make a good pitch and offer them at a competitive price, you can make a sale. However, here is the good part: When you make a sale, you will not make that much profit on that one sale, but you also get a customer that is very likely to return several times to your shop to buy more.

If you are dealing in this type of consumable, make sure to build a mailing list, so you can send out occasional reminders to your customers, so they will remember to come back to you when they need more. Offer special incentives (tenth order free, or something of that nature) to keep them coming back.

Finding It Locally

Now that you have decided on a category or two to focus on, you have to find it. Around your hometown there are resources that you may not realize exist. The advantage of local sourcing, too, is that you will save on shipping costs.

eBay sellers that deal in collectibles, antiques, arts, and crafts are especially adept at finding things locally. Start out by going to local crafts fairs, farmer's markets, flea markets, and church bazaars. These places are full of local craftspeople who make and sell beautiful items that would go very well on eBay. Of course, you do not want to pay their retail price, but remember, these people do not have a huge market and are always looking for a sale. Tell them about your eBay business and ask for a volume discount. It may well be that they have thought of selling on eBay but have not gotten around to it, do not have the time or inclination to do it themselves, or do not have a computer.

Yard sales are also occasional treasure troves of goodies, although you will find other sellers picking through local yard sales as well. Also, people in general have become more savvy about their goods since the popularity of eBay has skyrocketed, and people who would have had yard sales in the past are now selling their own attic full of junk on eBay themselves. Nonetheless, there are deals to be found there. Some yard sale enthusiasts will tell you that early in the mornings are the best time to go, before everything gets picked through, and there is some logic in that. However, there is also merit in going at the very end. You may miss out on some great products, but you will also be there to get the last-minute deals. People having yard sales do not want to pack up their stuff and haul it back inside, and you will have a very good chance of getting entire boxes full of goods for very little money. When you buy these end-of-sale boxes, they may contain some useless junk, but they will also contain some quality items you can sell and make the entire price very well worthwhile.

When you engage in local buying, you are bound to get people who hear about it and will constantly come around and offer you things. While sometimes you can actually get good deals this way, more often than not, these people have an inflated sense of what their item is really worth, so you will have to do some serious bargaining with them. On the other hand, they may just be looking for a few extra dollars, and you can get some good deals if you know what to look for and can separate the trash from the treasure.

I know of a couple down-and-out guys who, whenever they are in need of additional beer money, occasionally go around town, rooting through dumpsters and pulling out discarded odds and ends. They then take it to an acquaintance of theirs who deals on eBay and they attempt to sell these discards to her. Surprisingly, they are often successful. Now since I know the dumpster-divers and not the eBay seller in this case, I do not know how successful the seller is in making money with their findings, but I would assume that since she keeps on buying things from them that she has actually made some money. And to their credit, I know that they have come across some surprisingly nice finds. Of course, not everyone wants to drive through alleys picking through peoples' trash cans, but the story at least serves to point out the fact that you can find saleable items almost anywhere.

Finding It through Distributors

There are thousands of distributors out there, who offer large catalogs full of wholesale priced goods to people like flea marketers, craft show folk, and of course, eBay sellers. You can find many of these places on the Internet.

Some of these distributors are merely companies that re-distribute items from other distributors, and you must proceed with caution. Beware of advertisements that claim that you can re-sell their product at an exceptionally high profit. If they are selling an item to you for $5 a dozen, and their ad says "retail price $19.99 each!" then you may do best to move on to the next place. There are unrealistic claims out there.

Another thing to beware of when dealing with these sorts of wholesale distributors, especially if they are not local, is that the picture on the Web site may look much better than the actual product. If you are interested in a particular item, find out if you can buy just one first as a sample to inspect before placing a larger order. If they are not willing to sell you a single piece, that is a big red flag.

Last, while you may be able to find some good products at attractive wholesale prices from these distributors, there are thousands of others who are doing the same thing as you. These are stock items, and if you try to re-sell them on eBay, you may be very surprised to find that there are a hundred other people selling exactly the same thing.

Drop Shippers

Like the wholesale distributors, drop shippers also offer goods to thousands of resellers, many of them who deal on eBay. The advantage of a drop shipper though, is that you do not have to buy large quantities of any one product, and you do not have to worry about shipping. The drop shipper ships out the product on your behalf, using an address label that reflects the name of your own eBay shop.

The same warnings hold true here though. Beware of outrageous claims of unrealistic profit margins and try to buy one of the products yourself to inspect it before you start offering it.

eBay Arbitrage

A great place to find things to sell on eBay is, surprisingly, on eBay itself.

Surprised? Most people are. However, there are people who make a constant stream of good money by buying things off eBay, re-listing them, and selling them for a profit.

There is a trick to it, though. First, realize that there are different types of people who sell on eBay. There are professionals and people who are very familiar with their product line: people like you who want to make a profitable business out of it. Then there are people who are just selling things for fun, to clean out their attic, or just to get rid of all their junk. These are goods that they have already. They were not purchased for the express purpose of re-selling. Instead, these are things that they have acquired over the years and have already gotten some use out of. These goods are, therefore, for the seller, at the end of their useful life, so anything they get out of it is profit. That is why you may see someone selling a perfectly good second-hand item for $5, when another seller with a professional store may need to get $10 for the same thing.

In other words, if I buy an answering machine and use it for a year, then decide I do not need it anymore, and I sell it on eBay for $5, I would consider myself having made $5. However, if I have an answering machine store on eBay, I have to take into account my acquisition cost as well as the listing fees.

Find the occasional sellers who are just downsizing their possessions and you will get some deals. You may also find eBay sellers who just want to get out of the business, who tried it and failed, or just have too much stock. When you look for these types of sellers, you are getting the same sort of goods and same sort of deals that you would at a good yard sale. Then you can re-list the item and turn a profit!

Arthur and Margo Lemner

Art and Margo are collectors, who dealt mainly in vintage collectibles and fine art, such as photographs. "We sold on eBay for maybe two years, but not a high volume, only about a dozen items a month at most because of constraints on our time and the fact that posting auctions for one-of-a-kind items is fairly time consuming," Margo said. eBay was not their only sales outlet, however. They also sold some items to dealers at their shops or to dealers who were in town for antique shows. They also experimented with putting items on consignment at local thrift shops. In all, eBay accounted for about 25 percent of their selling.

On many a weekend day, you would be able to see them packing up their van to go "yard-saling" in the wee hours, eager to hit the sales when they first open. Most of the items they had to sell came from local yard sales, estate sales, rummage sales, and occasionally from thrift shops. However, Margo added a very relevant point about the popularity of eBay. It has made it more difficult to find these treasures. She adds, "Most of the second hand dealers sell on eBay themselves. They are unlikely to overlook items that might do well on eBay."

Pricing Strategies and Starting Bids

Beginning eBay sellers often just put items up for auction without a cohesive pricing strategy under the misguided belief that their item will be so much in demand that they will get far more than it is worth. This does not happen. In fact, if you do not plan your pricing strategy ahead of time, you are more likely to get less than what it is worth, you may lose money, and you will not be selling on eBay for very long.

No Minimum!

It is shocking from a business perspective how many items are out there with no reserve and no minimum bid. Without reserve pricing of some sort, you take a great risk. The practice of "sniping" will keep you from achieving a profit, and selling an item with no reserve and no minimum bid can be a very dangerous practice. It should be used only with extreme caution. Do not assume that there will be many bidders to drive up the price, or you could wind up selling that $500 antique for $1.

Also, do not assume that you must do business this way or nobody will bid. If your product has any value at all, putting a reserve or minimum bid amount on your listing will not hurt your chances at all. It is true that there are some buyers out there looking for extreme bargains and who will bid only on those things with no minimum. For the most part, they are other dealers looking to find something they can turn around for a quick profit.

If you end up selling half of the items you list for $1, you are going to lose money. Do not make the mistake of thinking that you can make it up on the shipping end. That does not work either. Buyers on eBay have gotten pretty savvy, and they are not going to fall for the high shipping cost routine. That was an early ploy, which some are still trying with very little success. This is where you sell an item at low cost, but then try to sneak in a "shipping and handling" charge that far exceeds your actual shipping costs.

There are a few cases where the no minimum strategy works, and that is if you know ahead of time that there will be serious bidders and there is a strong market for what you have. However, you have to be willing to take the risk of selling a product for less than what you need to get out of it!

Some sellers do use the $1 minimum bid strategy, even for items that cost far more, to avoid paying more in eBay listing fees. In addition, of course, the listing fees, if you do not manage them properly, can completely consume your profit margin, so this is a good thing to take into account. Nonetheless, you do not have to set your minimum bid at $1 if you think doing so may cause your item to be perceived as less valuable. If you feel that there will be a strong market for what you have, consider a starting bid somewhere close to your break-even point for selling. Study the listing fees and how they change based on the value of an item. Lowering your starting bid by a penny can sometimes save you money on your listing fees.

TIP: ONLY THE BEST

"Always strive to do better. Keep your eyes on your numbers. Do not let costs get away from you, but do not let profit be your only motive. Not every new client is worth signing, and not every buyer is out to rip you off. Do not tolerate second best. Your customers will not."

-Robert Sachs, RKS Solutions

The Fall of the Average Selling Price

A common lament among eBay sellers is that average selling prices seem to fall. "I just cannot get a good price for these things anymore," you say. Everybody else says that, too, yet, people still make a profit using eBay. The fact of the matter is that the eBay scene has changed since the early days, as does any sort of shopping venue. The fact is shopping venues change and mutate. It is their nature.

If you want to continue your success, you have to adopt your business to the inevitable changes. There is more competition on eBay, more stores selling the same things, and customers who are more sophisticated about acquiring goods inexpensively. When you first started out, you may have been able to get a high dollar for your goods and sell everything you put up. It is easy to make money when something is brand new and everybody wants it. However, what about that discount outlet at the old shopping mall? They make money a different way. They have adapted, and so to must you. eBay is no longer new, so people do not come just out of curiosity any more. They know it is there, they know how it works, and they use it when they need to buy something. But to a degree, eBay has lost its luster. It has gone from being a brand spanking new shopping mall to being a discount outlet.

That does not mean you cannot make money. You can. You can even make a great deal of money. You just have to go about it a little differently than you used to. In addition, your success now goes back to your product mix. Today, there are more eBay sellers selling the same thing, and so the natural law of supply and demand dictates that the average selling price will decrease. Spend more time in evaluating the items you put up, and do a little research to see how many other people are selling them. Make what you have interesting, make it stand out, and make it as unique as you possibly can.

At the same time, guard against driving down your own prices by flooding the market. Suppose you find an item that you sell almost immediately for a good profit. Your immediate logic would tell you that if you made good money from selling one, then you would make even better money if you sell a hundred of them. Despite the enormous number of visitors on eBay, it does not work that way. Smart buyers will wait you out believing, probably correctly, that you will not sell them all and will be forced to drop your price eventually. Keep your product mix constantly changing, and deal in smaller quantities whenever possible. The only time you should be dealing in very large quantities is when you have some sort of commodity oriented, consumable item like ink cartridges.

Second-Chance Offers

If you do have multiples of a particular item, you can sell them without having to create a separate listing for each one. A second-chance offer is a technique originally created to allow sellers to sell an item if the winning bidder does not pay. If this occurs, you can offer the next-highest bidder the product at the price they bid.

Not everybody knows, though, that even if your winning bidder does come through with the cash, you can still offer the same product (assuming you have multiples) to the losing bidders. Suppose, for example, that bidding started at $10 and the winning bid was $50. You ship the product to your winning bidder, but then calculate what price would have been your minimum acceptable bid. Suppose then that you figure that selling the product at $40 would still be profitable. In this case, say there were five bidders that bid in the $40 to $49 range, and so you can offer all five of those bidders the same product at the price they bid as well. The person who underbids will get a "second chance offer" e-mail, and in that e-mail there will be a link to a fixed-price listing, stating the price they bid, that will be visible only to that individual.

This type of strategy is actually preferable to the "Dutch" auction, because the second-chance offer gambit does not reveal to the buyers how many of the products you actually possess.

"Buy It Now"

Not everybody has the patience to wait around for an auction to end. In any retail environment, there is great value in capturing the sale when the shopper is most interested, which is when they first look at it and decide they want it. If they have to wait seven days to find out if they win the auction, they could lose interest. We are talking about the appeal of the "impulse buy." Give people something you know they want and give them the opportunity to buy it right now before they change their minds. That is why supermarkets keep candy and gossip magazines right at the checkout counter.

The "Buy It Now" option is a wonderful addition to eBay, and it adds an element of impulse purchase to the mix. Your "Buy It Now" strategy should be to set the "Buy It Now" price higher than your opening bid amount but still at a very competitive (but profitable) rate.

Reserve Price and Minimum Bid

Both of these prices serve the same purpose, and that is to avoid selling a product for less than what it is worth to you; however, they work a little differently. The reserve price option lets you set a minimum acceptable bid, but that minimum acceptable bid is not revealed to bidders. The "minimum bid" option, on the other hand, clearly states that bidding must start at that level. Some sellers prefer one to the other and have had success with both. However, some buyers balk at auctions with reserve prices built in, because they have no way of knowing how low they should start.

Dutch Auction

When you have multiples of a particular item, you can sell it with a Dutch auction format. In this technique, you set a minimum bid, shoppers say how many they want, and the highest price they will pay. At the end of the auction, all the bidders will pay the same price for the item, which is the amount of the lowest successful bid.

What this has the potential of doing is letting you sell your items for the lowest possible profit level, and in that respect, it does not go a long way toward making you the big money. If you have a great number of bidders on a Dutch auction, the lowest acceptable bid is very likely to be extremely close to the minimum bid that you have set. In most cases, the starting price is what goes, and in that respect, it really gives you very little advantage over just listing them in a fixed-price format.

Arthur and Margo Lemner,

eBay sellers have to be very sensitive to the profit margin, especially as the field heats up and more sellers enter the market. Profit margins naturally decrease as a result. Margo notes, "The profit margin depends on how valuable your items are. If they are inexpensive, you may spend a great deal of time making very little money. We have learned to avoid selling items that are too recent or too plentiful to be worth much to a collector. Also, if items do not sell after a second auction period, we usually withdraw them to avoid having the listing fees eat up all the profits. If you are selling regularly, you have a good idea of what the various fees will add up to, including the PayPal fee for receiving the payment.

"We determine prices partly based on our own knowledge of the quality, age, condition, and attractiveness of the item. The best source of pricing information is eBay itself. We check what similar items have sold for or not sold for in completed auctions. eBay used to make that information available for the month following the close of the auction in advanced searches. Now the period is only two weeks, which can make it more difficult to find a price for items that are relatively rare. This can be time consuming, however, because sometimes you have to read each auction description to know if the item is equivalent to the one you want to sell. We also use eBay pricing research to sell items on eBay and also to buy items from eBay."

Margo summarizes her success strategy. "Like any business, you have to put in time to be successful. You also have to work smart, not just work hard. You need to keep informed of any changes in eBay services or policies."

Branching Out

eBay may be a good tool for selling products, but it is not the only one. The most successful entrepreneurs never rely on a single venue, but instead sell their products through multiple sites, including other auction sites, online malls, and SEO-optimized Web sites. These other venues can be used either to make additional sales directly or to drive traffic to your eBay store.

eBay is a tool, and it is a good one. It is a tool that you use in your e-commerce initiatives to help you sell things. But does a carpenter have just a hammer in his toolbox? Does a plumber carry around a monkey wrench and nothing else? Not if they are any good. And you too, should not limit yourself only to one tool.

There are more tools out there that you can use in your business, and they will help you become much more successful in the end. Like the carpenter's tools, each tool in your own retail toolbox will help you do different things.

The Online Auction Business

When you think of an online auction, chances are, you think of eBay first. To be sure, eBay is by far the largest. However, eBay is not the only one. Online auctions are big business, and there are other generalized auction venues like eBay, as well as more specialized ones that focus on particular product types, such as antique auctions or auctions for business services.

You may have made some good money on eBay, and you have a certain sense of loyalty to the company, but that should not mean that you should restrict yourself. Branching out into other online auction venues may well expand your business significantly. Even if eBay remains your largest producer, having two or three smaller producing auction sites can go a long way toward helping you achieve a financial goal. In the world of business, more is usually better.

There are some very good arguments for diversifying into other online auctions. While you should not give up on eBay entirely, there are some other auctions that may be more specialized and may be very well-suited to a particular product line that you carry. A specialized auction site will have more savvy shoppers who are familiar with the real value of what you are offering. And while everybody loves a bargain no matter where they are shopping, you are less likely to have your site bombarded by bargain-hunters who want to buy your $1,000 first edition book for $1.50.

Here Are a Few Alternative Auction Sites:

Amazon.com: No, you do not have to be a big publishing company to sell things on Amazon. It has, in fact, become a popular place for small-time book dealers to sell second-hand and rare books. It is not an auction site actually. Instead, you list your items for a fixed price. We usually associate Amazon with books, and that was how it first got started in the business, as a large online book dealer. But today, you can buy and sell just about anything on **Amazon.com.**

It is easy to get started on **Amazon.com** as a seller, and you will notice on the home page that there is a link that says, "Sell Your Stuff." That link will take you to an information page that tells you everything you need to know. Like eBay, you also make a description of the product you have to sell, set a price, and register with Amazon Payments so you can collect your money. There is a closing fee that varies, a per transaction fee of 99 cents, plus a percentage of the sales price. The good news is that you get 60 days worth of listing time, and if the item does not sell, you do not have to pay anything. If you do not just want to sell a few odd items, you can become a Pro Merchant. Pro Merchant listings do not close after 60 days, and you save a little money on listing fees since Pro Merchants do not have to pay the 99 cent listing fee.

Also, just as on eBay, you can create your own online shop on **Amazon.com**. And if you are just hopelessly addicted to the auction format, **Amazon.com** does offer auctions, although they are less well-known than their straight sale option.

Ubid.com: This is one to watch. Rapidly becoming very popular as an alternative to eBay, **Ubid.com** gives you the enormous advantage of not having to pay listing fees. If you are drowning in eBay fees and are not selling a high percentage of everything you list, you definitely want to consider Ubid. Simply stated, if it does not sell, you do not pay. You pay based on a percentage of the winning bid amount, which varies from 2.5 percent to 12.5 percent. However, **Ubid.com** is a bit less of an open marketplace, and participants must be certified sellers. If you are a casual seller who has not yet established a legitimate business entity (which you should have done already, if you are interested enough to be reading this book), you are not allowed on **Ubid.com**.

Yahoo.com: Yes, it is still free. It is unbelievable, but true, and it has been free since June 2005. Yahoo is a strong competitor to eBay, and as one of the top search portals, it generates traffic. Your listing is not quite as detailed as eBay, but then again, it is free. You do get the basics: you can describe your product, upload photographs of it, and you do have an "About Me" page that you can use to describe your business and create an extra little sales pitch. It is also easy for a visitor to click a button to see all of your offerings at once.

Of course, nothing is entirely free, and the price you pay for getting the free listing is that Yahoo places a small strip of text ads alongside the right side of your auction listing. Whether this distracts from your auction is highly debatable, but it seems to be worth it. You get a free listing, and Yahoo gets to place ads. You may lose traffic as some people exit your listing page to visit one of the paid ads, but that is part of the risk. Remember, you are not paying anything for the listing anyway. Therefore, you can afford to lose a small percentage of traffic.

Typically, the number of people who exit through one of these text ads is very small, so you have nothing to worry about. This may be a great venue for testing out new items, or even for selling items that did not sell on the first round on eBay. This one is definitely worth the time; check it out and give it a try. You have nothing to lose.

There are many more out there as well. The advertiser-supported, free auction format is actually gaining some significant ground, and there are several smaller auction sites that offer free listings in exchange for placing Google AdSense ads on your listing page. The bottom line here is that you should expand your auction listing presence outside of eBay. You may be quite surprised as to what you can get. If nothing else, you will have a good stable of venues for selling your unsold items.

Sell Online Direct

An auction site, whether it is eBay or one of the others, does not have to be your primary means of sales. Many vendors have great success creating their own e-commerce Web site and offering products for sale directly. Your own site can be a wonderful supplement to your eBay presence, and you can establish a two-way referral between your eBay store and your own e-commerce store.

The best strategy is to use your own e-commerce storefront to sell other items that are not on eBay but are in the same general category. That way, you will continue to get cross-traffic, as people look for more items as they shop. Another advantage is that if you are running your own storefront, you are not paying anybody any listing fees, and you can list a product there indefinitely. It is great for listing products that have not sold on eBay. After one re-listing on eBay, unless it is a very unusual and expensive item, it is usually time to give it up. The cost of three listings on eBay for any given product is probably going to eat your profits, and then it is time to move that product to one of the free auction sites, or in this case, to your own e-commerce storefront site.

There are several different ways to create your own e-commerce site, and there are plenty of ready-made templates available that make the set-up easy. There is a little more involved here than just listing a product on an auction site, since you have to take care of everything yourself, including the back-end financials. You have to set up a method of accepting credit card payments.

Setting up your own e-commerce Web site takes a few steps, and there have been several books written about the subject, so we will not attempt to get into all the details here. But briefly, here is what is involved:

1. Get a credit card merchant account or use a service.

2. Obtain hosting space (usually very inexpensive).

3. Create your Web site, from scratch or using a template.

4. List your site on all the major search engines.

5. Cross-promote your site with your other online presences.

You will no doubt find several free Web hosting services, but if you are attempting to create a professional site, pass these by. You will not be able to do some of the things you need to do in terms of providing credit card services, and you will be very limited as to space and bandwidth.

It does not cost that much to have a good, professional Web hosting service host your site, and it is well worth the money. Another advantage to using a paid hosting service as opposed to a free one is that you can create your own domain. This just makes you look more professional. A shopper is more likely to go to Bob's Printer Shop at **www.bobsprintershop.com** than they would visit a site that sports a longer URL, like **www.geocities.yahoo.com/bobsprinters.com**.

Festivals, Fairs, and Flea Markets

Yes, it is quite a departure from selling online, but it is still definitely something worth considering. Every community has these little events, and some vendors make big money at them. You register, pay a fee, and set up a table and display your products.

However, this can be a great adjunct to your eBay business, and a great way to promote it. These events are often very crowded. Thousands of people may walk by your table in a day. You will naturally make some sales, but perhaps even more importantly, you can also direct people to your eBay business. There will be plenty of people who like what you have displayed, but do not want to buy that day, are short on cash, or just cannot make up their mind. Directing them to your eBay site will give them an option other than waiting until the next festival to see you again.

Have a stack of brochures, fliers, or attractive post cards with a picture of your goods on them and give these out liberally to everyone that stops, or even pauses, in front of your table. This printed material should give a brief description of your business, have contact information, and should tell the URL of your eBay store (and any other online presences you may have). In addition, create a large sign that can be seen from a distance, saying something to the effect of "Visit me online at eBay!" Doing so not only encourages passers-by to check you out online, it also lends you a bit of instant credibility. Shoppers at the festival will of course, recognize eBay, and will know instantly that you are not just a hobbyist. You are a pro.

Creating a "Sticky" Site

There is more to selling on eBay than putting up products on your site. You must create an individual identity for yourself and your eBay store that will be memorable. You do not want your customers to say to people, "I bought this beautiful necklace from eBay." You want them to say, "I bought this beautiful necklace from Billy Bob's eBay store." Granted, that is hard to achieve. eBay itself has tremendous name recognition, and the natural tendency of shoppers is to say simply, "I bought it on eBay." But if you do your homework and play it the right way, they just might remember to come back to your store the next time they visit eBay.

The best customer is an old customer. New ones are great too, but the customer that keeps coming back is worth far more. That is why marketers of all sorts, whether they are selling on the Internet, through direct mail, at a corner store, or at the local flea market, go to great lengths to give their customers a reason to come back. Some online stores make over half of their profits from return business.

It is a natural tendency to get into the habit of buying certain things at certain stores. I have a certain place where I like to buy my green tea. It is a little Asian market run by a Vietnamese family. If I looked around long and hard enough, I would probably find another place that has just as good a deal, or maybe even for a few cents cheaper, but like most consumers, I am lazy. Besides, I have been there many times and have always been treated well so I trust them. The owner recognizes me when I walk in, and I speak a few words to him in Vietnamese. If I go in by myself, his wife will ask me, "Where's your wife today?" and maybe we will exchange stories about spending lazy days along the Mekong River.

That store owner has it down. I do not know if he has ever read any books about marketing, but he has the concept of generating return business down cold. He knows almost everybody that ever goes into his store, takes time to listen to his or her stories, and tells his as well. Many of his customers are immigrants, and he knows where everybody is from. When I go there on Fridays, I will hear at least four or five different languages being spoken by his customers from Vietnam, Laos, Cambodia, and Thailand. He makes them feel at home.

Besides just greeting everyone, he makes them feel at home and keeps them coming back with his product mix as well. If you have ever been in a Southeast Asian kitchen, you know that fish sauce is a vital ingredient in many dishes. It is basic, and it is made by grinding up fish, straining out the juice, and fermenting it. It has been manufactured and bottled in almost every Asian country, and they have exported it. Fish sauce from a company in Thailand is pretty much the same as fish sauce from a company in Vietnam. It all has fermented fish juice. There is really not much difference. Nonetheless, he carries fish sauce from no less than four different manufacturers in four different Asian countries. Why? Because when my wife, who is from Thailand, went in there for the first time, she saw the brand of fish sauce she used to buy back home, and it brought a smile to her face. And so we go there every week, so she can get authentic fish sauce and other authentic products from Thailand. That, dear readers, is the art of keeping 'em coming back.

In the online world, you can do it too. And a big part of it is creating what is called a "sticky site." No, it is not sticky because somebody spilled fish sauce all over it. "Sticky" means that people keep wanting to return to that particular site in the same way my wife wants to keep coming back to the little Vietnamese market.

You can translate this same experience into your eBay site or other e-commerce site. Do the same thing. Treat your customers in a friendly manner, know their names, and go out of your way to take good care of them. Get them what they want, help them find it, and make sure you let them know about next week's specials.

The Little Extras

The Asian market keeps people coming back because he does things that he does not really have to do. From a practical point of view, importing fish sauce from four different countries is probably extra trouble, especially for a product that is almost identical regardless of its origin. But it makes his Thai customers happy to see the kind they are used to. In your Web site, you can add the little extras as well.

One way to add these little extras is to offer high quality

information. If you sell Asian antiques, for example, you probably have a good audience of collectors already, but you can give them a little more with their Ming vase. Give them a short story of how you acquired the product, and tell a personal tale of how you bought it from a woman who claimed to be 105 years old and attributed her longevity to chewing betel nuts.

Besides personal stories, which make the visit nicer and make the product more interesting, you must also give them some practical information. If they are buying a Ming vase, they may want to know something about the Ming dynasty. Take some time to do some research, write a short essay about it, and about the artwork of the period. Provide some links to some authoritative sites for further information.

Remember that people use the Web not just for finding things to buy, but to an even larger degree, for finding information and doing research. When somebody wants information about Asian antiques, they may well be led to your site through various links or a search engine that has picked up your articles and essays. They go there to read the information and they stay to buy the vase.

Shoppers like to get a little extra from their experience. That is not always easy to do in the online world, and that is why shopping centers and malls will never completely go away. Sure, I could buy green tea online, but it is not nearly as much fun as going to the little Asian store downtown.

You can come as close as you possibly can to a friendly in-person visit by remembering to provide a few things on your Web site:

- **Get personal.** Remember to include a friendly "About Me" page with a few personal anecdotes and maybe even a picture.

- **Where did it come from?** Do not just say that you have a beautiful antique Khmer-style oil lamp. Tell the visitor a little about the Cambodian bazaar where you found it and what it was like to be there.

- **What is its history?** Become an authority figure. In addition to listing the product and telling about where you got it, provide information about its history. Make yourself available to answer questions from people doing research on the subject. When somebody comes up with a question about a product category you deal in, the person will think of you and visit your site to find the answer.

Be the Center of Your Community

I lived in Albuquerque for a brief time, and there was a particular restaurant I liked to visit every day called the Frontier Restaurant. Centered across from the university, over the years it had become a hangout, not just for students, but also for writers, activists, and people with nothing better to do than to sit there, drink coffee, and tell stories all day. You could post a notice on the bulletin board, and if you had some sort of political or special interest group, no matter how off-the-wall it was, you could meet in one of the back rooms for free. I kept regular hours there and people knew where to find me. If I was not there, the server would be able to let them know where I was.

Although it was really just a restaurant, it had become a de facto community center of sorts. I could walk into that restaurant any time of the day, and I would always see somebody I knew. In fact, one day I returned after being away for a few years, walked into the Frontier, and my old friend Ron, a Cajun man with stories of his own to tell, was sitting there, just as if he had never left. The Frontier was just that sort of place, where everybody knew everybody, and you would go there not just for coffee, but for information and conversation as well.

This is not something you can do directly on your eBay store site, but you can do it on your other sites. On the Internet, people want something for nothing. They want service, and they want freebies. You can give it to them.

One thing that keeps people coming back is an online discussion forum. The online forum has become the cyber version of the coffeehouse hangout, and you can use it to your benefit. This is easy to set up and can be done without much of an investment. If you deal in a specific type of product, antique, or category, and there are many people interested in it, they may form a community. That community may as well be centered on your Web site. Again, if you are the one who sells Asian antiques, all the people who are interested in them really like to talk about them. You can provide them with that forum.

Now it is true, you are not going to make money directly from providing a discussion forum on your Web site. In addition, it will be a little bit of extra trouble to maintain it. But it will be an indirect money-maker for you, because your site will become much better known, and your site will also come to be the ultimate authority on the subject. Not everybody who visits the forum will buy anything, but some will. And those who do not, may know somebody who does want to buy something, and of course, they will refer them to your site.

eBay's Discussion Boards

eBay itself has a very robust discussion forum and a lively community of people who meet in cyberspace to discuss their businesses and their lives. There are several different categories of discussions that you can join. Of course, you do not use these forums to promote your sites, but you can nonetheless participate for the purpose of making yourself known.

If you become known on the discussion boards as someone who is very knowledgeable about a particular subject, you may well get many people looking for your online store just because they read a comment you made on a discussion board. Take some time to become active in these discussions, and in no time, you will become known as an authority.

Other Ways to Keep 'Em Coming Back

In addition to some of the techniques described in this chapter, the following are a few basic tips that drive return business:

1. **Provide great customer service.** Make sure your customers get their products on schedule and in good condition, and make yourself available for any questions or follow-ups they may have.

2. **Personalized marketing.** By keeping a database of previous purchases, you can get a good idea of what each customer likes, and you can use that information to create custom, highly targeted e-mail campaigns where you send customers links to items that match their customer profile.

3. **Personalized newsletters.** Create an opt-in newsletter that your customers can subscribe to. Include valuable information and commentary in the newsletter, as well as information about your latest offerings.

4. **Promotional gifts and discounts.** Include specials. If you sell consumable items, for example, offer a "tenth order free" deal or something of that nature.

CHAPTER 20

Search Engine Optimization and PPC Ads

You can promote your eBay store and other affiliated sites by optimizing them for search engines and purchasing PPC ads to drive traffic.

What Is PPC?

Pay-per-click (PPC) is a type of online advertising where you maintain strict control over your spending, and you pay only when somebody actually clicks on your ad. One of the most popular PPC programs is Google AdWords, and it is very cost-effective. The ad is very simple, and you can create it yourself. There are no graphics involved. It is just text. You have probably seen these ads before. They take the form of a small strip of text ads, usually alongside a page of text, and it says "Ads by Google" in small text.

You can get started for a small amount of money. It does not take much to promote your eBay store online. It works on a bid basis. You bid against certain keywords for having your ad show higher than other ads in the same category. Your ad will show up in two places: on the Google search results when somebody searches on one of your keywords, and on individual Web sites that are relevant to your keywords. You decide how much you will pay for each keyword, and you decide on a maximum amount to spend per day. You can easily get started and test the waters by bidding five or ten cents on a keyword, and putting a limit of two or $3 a day. If it works, you can experiment from there with different bid levels and maximums to see how much you get in the way of results.

You start by getting an AdWord account. You can sign up in just a few minutes. There is not much involved. You will be approved in a couple days after Google checks the contents of your site. There are no requirements regarding traffic volume. They just want to visit sites to eliminate certain types of content from their network. Chances are, so long as your site is not offensive and does not contain pornography, you are in.

Once you are approved, the next step is to create your first campaign. You get a headline, two lines of text, and a URL link. That is just a few words, so you have to be very economical in writing your text. You can create as many campaigns as you want, testing the waters with different combinations of keywords, different bid levels, and different ads.

Your ads start appearing almost immediately after you create your first campaign, and you may get some results the first day!

When you are creating your campaign, be sure to set a daily maximum spend limit. If you do not, you may wind up spending more than you anticipated.

How Search Engines Work

Almost everyone who uses the Web has used a search engine. In fact, the Google search engine is one of the most common starting portals in the world. However, your site does not just show up, you have a little work to do.

Search engines work by using a software engine called a "spider." This engine constantly searches through the entire Web, finding new sites as well as sites that have been updated since the last time the spider read it. When the spider hits a Web site, it indexes it. In other words, it creates an index that contains all the words on each page, including any headers. It calculates how frequently a particular word is found, how close to the beginning of the page it occurs, and dozens of other factors. Based on a complicated algorithm, the spider will determine how relevant each given site is to a particular keyword. That is how a search engine knows that a site that is dedicated exclusively to Beanie Babies is more relevant than one that just mentions them in passing, and the engine will put the dedicated site nearer the top of the search results.

How Search Engine Optimization Works

There is a school of thought that holds that so long as your Web site is well written and on subject, you do not have to do anything else. The spider will find it, see what the site is about, and place it appropriately. Those who follow this school believe that you do not have to alter your writing style in any way to artificially "beef up" the spider results.

Unfortunately, it does not work that way. Remember, there are millions of Web sites out there, and you are competing with plenty of other sites that are about the same subject as yours. You need to give yourself an edge through any legitimate means possible. Of course, in a perfect world of good writing, this would not be necessary, but this is not a perfect world.

Before you start writing, make a short list of your most relevant keywords. Do not just limit yourself to one keyword, remember that people may use different words, phrases, or combinations of words to find you. Somebody that wants to buy a seung, a traditional Siamese musical instrument, may search under the word "seung," or they may just search on the phrases "Siamese musical instrument," "traditional Thai instrument," or "Asian stringed instrument." You will want to make sure to use all of the key phrases in your text.

Always use your main keyword in the very first sentence of your text as well as in the headline and page title. Within the first paragraph, try to work in a mention of each of your major keywords and phrases. Sprinkle them liberally throughout the entire text, without making it sound awkward.

The Invisible Header

Your Web site creation software will give you an opportunity to create a special type of page header called a "META tag." This tag is not seen in the results when a visitor goes to your page, but the search engine's spider will see it, even if nobody else will. You include the META tag only for the spider's benefit. Within this META tag, you enter in every relevant keyword, key phrase, and combination you can think of, just for good measure, including misspelled ones. In the above example, in your META tag you might also include "soong" in addition to "seung," since the Thai alphabet does not translate directly to the English alphabet, and people may search on either spelling.

This is not just a tool for your external Web sites; you can use the META tag on eBay as well. Be sure to submit your "About Me" page and your eBay store to the major search engines so they will pick it up!

Besides the META tag, you will also have an opportunity, on any type of Web site including your eBay site, to include a META description. The META description is a little different from the META tag. The META tag is meant to be seen only by the search engine spider for giving you an indexing advantage. The META description, on the other hand, appears in the search results when people search on a keyword that you have specified.

The META description does not actually appear on your Web site when somebody visits it, but it does appear on the page of search results. Usually short, between 20 and 30 words, the META description tag will tell the search engine to put those words under the page title in the search results. If you do not include a META description, the engine will just pick up the first couple of lines of text on your page and show that. The advantage of the META description is that you can tailor the search results list to encourage people to come to your site with a very precise description of what your site is about.

Submit to Search Engines

As I mentioned, the search spider constantly surfs the entire Web and will eventually come across your site. But to optimize your results, do not wait for the spider to drop by to visit. You have to invite the spider to your site.

There are services that will charge you to submit your listings to all the search engines, but you can just as easily do it yourself at no cost. The services may tout that they can list your site with "hundreds" of search engines, but in fact, the top three—Google, MSN, and Yahoo—comprise almost all the search volume and the others are not nearly as relevant. All three of those search engines have simple instructions online for submitting a site. Submit your site only once to each portal, and do not submit individual eBay listings, only your "About Me" page and your eBay store. Constantly submitting individual listings will cause the search engines to think you are just SPAMming, and they will ignore you.

Google Sitemap

The Google portal is probably the most important of the three, simply because it is by far the largest. Some people find that it takes weeks or even months for their site to appear on Google, especially when they are first starting out. You can speed this up by taking advantage of a free Google service called "Google Sitemaps." You simply create a sitemap to your Web site, and upload it to your server. This is not the same thing as the sitemap that is visible on your Web site, which just shows links to all of your pages for the benefit of your site's visitors. This is a different sitemap that is not visible to your visitors. It is visible only to Google. Again, it is created solely for the benefit of the Google spider.

The purpose of the Google sitemap is to allow the spider to identify the pages of your site. Google encourages its use because it speeds up the process and takes a burden off their spider. Google explains the process at **http://www.google.com/webmasters/sitemaps.** If your site is small (under a hundred pages or so), there are some free third party sitemap generators you can use. I use one that can be found at **http://www.xml–sitemaps.com. It does all** the work of creating the sitemap for you, in the exact format required by Google.

Cross Links

Another way the search engine determines how relevant or how important your site is to any given search is to determine how many other sites are linking to yours. The logic here is that if there are a hundred sites linking to your site, you probably know what you are talking about, and you will get a higher spot in the search results.

Now before you go out and get a hundred other people to exchange links with you, slow down a little bit. It is not that easy. The search engine will also examine the quality and relevancy of the sites linking to you. That is why all those link exchange programs are not as valuable as they seem. Establishing a good network of cross-links takes time, but it will happen, sometimes without your even trying. I have some Web sites that have 40 or 50 links to high quality sites just because they referred to it as an authoritative site when discussing a subject. Links may also turn up in discussion forums. Of course, you will meet other eBay sellers along the way, and you may want to exchange links with them, so long as what they sell does not directly compete with what you sell.

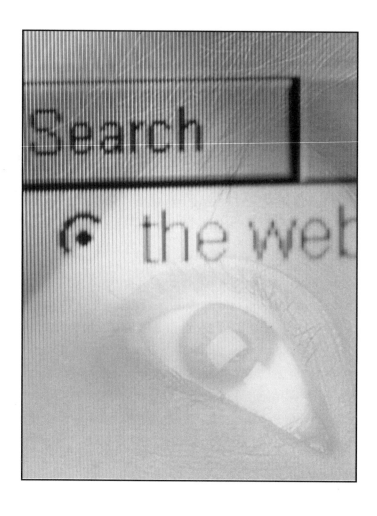

Optimizing eBay Search

Out of 80 million searches that are made on eBay every day, how can you make sure that people are finding what you have to sell? Just as you optimize your content to achieve the best results with general Google searches, you must also optimize your content and listings to achieve the greatest results within eBay itself.

There are many ways to make sure that people searching on eBay find what you are offering. The first step, however, is to become familiar with the buyer's end of the process.

Before you start selling on eBay, you should have already become a buyer. Spend some time just surfing eBay, using the search functions, and finding what you like. Take notice of what works and what does not when trying to find something. Try to find an item using different keywords, and see where the same item comes up in the search results using different keyword searches.

eBay Keyword Marketing

We have talked about Google keyword text ads previously, and this is a great way to get exposure. But what some people do not realize is that eBay has a keyword marketing program of its own as well.

The eBay Keywords program (**http://eBay.admarketplace.net**) will drive traffic to your auctions and eBay store and help increase your visibility overall. You do not have to have a big marketing budget, either. Here is how it works. It is very much like the Google program. You create text ads or banner ads, and they appear on the search results that appear when a buyer performs a search using specific keywords that match the keywords you have attached to your ad. You can link an ad to a specific auction or to your eBay store. Some novice eBay sellers make the mistake of thinking that they are not eligible to participate in this program or that it would be too expensive. Nothing could be further from the truth. Anybody can participate, and it is very inexpensive. You do not have to have a big budget, and you do not have to be a Powerseller to take advantage of this great program.

You only have to pay if somebody clicks on the ad, and you can impose a budget for your campaign. Like the Google AdWords program, you bid on clicks, and specify the maximum amount of money you are willing to pay for each click, and the maximum amount of money you want to spend in any given day. You can start a campaign with as little as $20. And as an added benefit, if your ad is linked to a specific auction, your campaign will be automatically paused when the auction is over, so you do not waste any money paying for clicks for something that has already been sold.

This takes a little thought, and besides creating an effective ad, you also must attach a good selection of keywords. This is what determines where and when the ad shows up. Remember that people may not always use the same keyword you would when searching for an item. Using only one or two keywords is going to limit your results.

If you are creative, you can go beyond the simple text ad and create your own graphic ad that includes a picture or logo.

When you use this eBay tool, you bid on keywords, and the bidding starts at ten cents per click and goes up in increments of a penny. You do not have to have the highest bid to have your ad shown. You just have to have the highest bid to have it on the top. With that in mind, your bidding strategy does not necessarily have to be to outbid everyone else. You can have a very successful pay-per-click campaign just by keeping your clicks in the top ten. It is a bit tricky to find the best amount to bid, but the best way to find out is with a little trial and error. Start your click bid at ten cents and go up from there in small increments of a penny or two. Be sure to keep a cap on how much you want to spend every day because if you happen to hit the top bid, you may end up spending more than you should.

Having the top bid is not always the best strategy. You may end up spending more on pay-per-click than you are earning from profit on the item you are advertising. The person at the top may get a thousand clicks and you may get only ten, but then again, that ten clicks may be more than enough for your particular purpose. Your goal in pay-per-click is to be able to pay the least amount possible per click while getting just the right amount of results.

When you are creating your eBay text ad or banner ad, be very specific. eBay shoppers are often looking for something in particular, so try to communicate about either a specific item that you have on offer or a category of items. An ad for "Dan's Cool Stuff on eBay" will not get many clicks, but an ad for "Dan's Asian Antiquities" will get you some shoppers who are looking for something in particular.

If you decide to go with a graphical banner instead of a text ad, eBay has some specific guidelines as to how it should look. The size is 468 by 60 pixels, and you must create it in GIF format. eBay frowns on animation in ads, so do not put in any of those annoying, flashing, spinning things. True, they get attention, but nobody likes them!

After you have created your ad and specified your keywords, you will be shown some competing ads for the same keyword, and you will have a chance to see what other people are bidding for the same keyword. This information will give you a good idea of where you should start your bidding. You do not have to have a single bid price for all keywords. You can adjust bids to match the popularity of each keyword. Also, remember that you will not necessarily pay the highest amount you specify. For example, if you specify a bid of 25 cents for a particular keyword, that does not mean you will pay the full 25 cents each time your ad is clicked. It works on a proxy basis, so your keyword bid is increased in one-cent increments up until the maximum specified.

Front Page Exposure

You may have noticed that on eBay's home page, there are several categories and subcategories of products. These categories change regularly, and you can get the greatest exposure simply by timing your auctions to match these categories.

You can find out what categories are going to be listed in future weeks by visiting the eBay Merchandising Calendar. This calendar will show you a schedule of which categories will be featured on this home page in the future weeks. Study this calendar on a regular basis. The best time to list an item is when that item's category is going to be featured on this category list on the home page.

Have a Featured Auction

The "Featured Auction" listing gives you an incredible amount of visibility, but it is something to be used sparingly because of the cost involved. Simply put, when you buy this option, your auction is listed above all other auctions in its given category. There are two ways you can have a featured auction. The Featured Plus! Option, which costs $19.95, will put your listing at the top of the list. You also have a chance of having your auction displayed in eBay's "Featured Items" section of other category pages, but this is completely random. The second option is much more expensive, and this is the Home Page Featured Auction listing. For $39.95 ($79.95 for multiple quantity listings), your item will appear at the top of the eBay "Featured Items" page. eBay also will select at random some of these to appear on the eBay home page.

This is, of course, about the best exposure you can buy from eBay, but it is not cheap and should be used only for items that are going to bring in top dollar.

Find Out If It Is Working

You have optimized your keywords on eBay and taken advantage of all the features eBay has to offer. How do you know if it is working? The obvious way, of course, is simply to track your sales. Naturally, if you are spending a fortune on pay-per-click eBay ads and "Featured Item" listings, and you are not making any sales, you are wasting your time. But it goes beyond that. Sometimes the sales are coming in, but it is hard to get a handle on whether those ads are working and how effective your keyword strategy is.

A simple hit counter is the next step, and these are widely available often at no charge in the form of freeware or shareware. The counter will give you a better idea of how many times your auction listing is being visited. However, even this is limited. While it is useful, it just counts how many times a page is viewed. It does not give you any deeper statistics. It does not distinguish between visitors. A count of ten hits may be ten separate visitors, or it may be one person going back to see the same page ten times.

Beyond that, there are third-party tools such as the ones found at sites like Sellathon, **www.sellathon.com,** that provide you with detailed, real-time information about how each visitor found your site, whether they used a search tool and which search terms they used to find you, which category they browsed on eBay to find your page, and how they sorted their search results. It can also tell you whether a visitor is watching your auction and a wealth of other details. It is simple to use. You just use the provided tracking code and cut and paste it onto your auction page.

eBay Keywords

The keywords you use in both your eBay advertising and within the eBay listing itself will make or break you. The keywords determine whether your auction will show up when somebody is doing a search. Here are a few things to keep in mind:

- **Use both keywords and key phrases.** In addition to using single-word keywords, use phrases as well. Sometimes people will search on a phrase that will be made up of two, three, or more words. If you are able to match that phrase, you will have a better chance of getting on the top of their results list than if you match only a single word.

- **Avoid "keyword spamming."** You may be tempted to put in many keywords that are not related or are only very marginally related to what you have to offer to try to get the most clicks. It does not work. You need to keep it relevant. Use many keywords to be sure, but make sure that every one you use is relevant to your products.

Keywords In Titles

Besides just listing the keywords separately when you make your listing, keep keywords in mind when you are writing your titles as well. Make your title precise and descriptive to increase your chances of showing up in more results lists. Try to use keywords in the title as much as possible. If you can manage it without sounding awkward, try to use both a keyword and a key phrase in the title.

For example, suppose you have an antique Khmer oil lamp for sale. What are the main keywords that people may be searching on to find such a thing? If you create a title that says simply, "Khmer oil lamp," you will get some search hits, but not as many as if you would use more descriptors. People looking for this item may be searching using key phrases like "Asian antiques," "Asian art," or "Cambodian pottery." Incorporate at least one of these additional key phrases into your title to come up with something like "Antique Asian Khmer oil lamp from 17th Century Cambodia."

Customer Service

Just because you have an Internet business does not mean everything has to be automated. Providing excellent, personalized customer service is essential and will help build a larger base of returning customers.

The greatest mistake ever made when starting an Internet business of any sort, including an eBay business, is to think that because it is online, you can remove yourself from the equation and become anonymous. I have encountered too many people who want to start an Internet business, but they do not list their address, phone, or contact information saying, "I do not want to be bothered," or "I do not want a bunch of people calling me at all hours." Well, the fact of the matter is, you are in business. Part of the deal is that you are going to be bothered, and people will call you at all hours. Accept it and get used to it. Nobody ever said making money was convenient or easy. If you go out of your way to become inaccessible, you will not get as much business. It is that simple. Yes, you will get the occasional midnight call, and once in a while somebody who is just crazy. It is all part of the package. If you cannot deal with that, then go to work for somebody else.

Your Working Hours

Part of the attraction of working for yourself is that you get to choose your own hours. Well, in a way. You will quickly find out that it is not as easy as you thought, and ultimately, you will work harder being self-employed than you ever did "working for the man." While it is true that you will have more flexibility, you will still have deadlines to meet, packages to get out on time to meet commitments to customers, and more than likely, you will find yourself creating a schedule for yourself.

True enough, if you are not a "morning" person, you can goof off until noon and then work until 8 p.m. if you want. It does not matter really, so long as you meet your commitments and make yourself available. For me, having been self-employed for the past 15 years, I often find myself taking calls and sending out e-mails at all hours of the day from early morning until late at night. When I am at my winter home in Bangkok, which is 12 hours ahead of Eastern Time, I may take calls at 3 a.m. to accommodate customers in the United States. Strange, since I wanted to work for myself because I thought it would be easier. I was wrong about that.

Regardless of how you arrange your workday, it is best from an organizational point of view if you apply some measure of regularity to it, and most importantly, meet your deadlines. You may decide that you prefer to work only on Tuesdays, Wednesdays, and Thursdays, and if your business is not that big, that may certainly be adequate. But there is one caveat there. On your days off, which would be Sunday, Monday, Friday, and Saturday, there will still be e-mails coming in. Orders will be arriving in your e-mail box. People may be calling you, wondering if you could find a particular item for them.

And these people must be accommodated. That is why even on your days off, you will do well to spend an hour answering your e-mails and taking care of things that need an immediate response.

Expectations

Among all businesses, online or otherwise, eBay has perhaps the highest expectations of good service than any other. Buyers know that they can demand it and expect it. They know that if an eBay seller provides poor service, they will get a negative feedback, and after a few negative feedbacks, that seller will be out of business.

The feedback system is a bit unforgiving, but it is the way eBay operates. Every business at one time or another has probably had a dissatisfied customer, but eBay is the only one that allows those dissatisfied customers to post their complaints where all the other customers can see. When you go to the grocery store and the bagger puts your bread on the bottom of the bag and crushes it, the manager may give you another loaf of bread, but he certainly would not let you write in marker on the front window, "My bread was crushed here. Avoid checkout lane six." eBay is the only business I know of that allows this sort of public feedback. It is no skin off eBay's nose either way, because it is not eBay that will be put out of business. It is the eBay seller. There are millions of sellers. One less will not make any difference.

It is precisely this brutal feedback system that has raised customer expectations. With eBay, the customer has tremendous power, far more power than with any other sales venue. As an eBay seller, you have to work within this framework, and customer service has to be a high priority for you.

Responding To E-Mails

If you have good items up for auction, chances are you will get at least a few e-mails asking questions for nearly every item you have. First, try to respond to these e-mails as quickly as you can. Never take more than 24 hours to respond. Ideally, you should check your e-mails and send out responses several times a day. Often, since auctions are listed with items with the ending time ending soonest, buyers may not even see your auction until the last day of the sale. On that last day, you will get the most action, and you are very likely to get e-mail questions up until a few hours of the auction's closing. If you have auctions closing soon, check for e-mails frequently.

If you still have a day job and cannot check your eBay business's e-mail during the day, make note of this in your "About Me" page and with your listing. A simple note to the effect of, "e-mails will be answered promptly between the hours of 5 p.m. and 10 p.m. daily" will suffice.

It does not have to take as long as you might think. Over time, you will see patterns in the e-mail queries, and you can develop "stock" answers. While you do not want to send a completely cut-and-paste form letter addressed to "dear customer," you can certainly have a set of cut-and-paste responses that you can use. The trick here is to create e-mails and templates that you can use to create responses that are both customized and personalized at the same time. Address the person by name every time. Paste in the appropriate "stock" response, but then take a moment to look it over to make sure it fits. You may need to tweak a word or a sentence here or there to make sure it is appropriate. In this way, you are able to send a response that is quick, personalized, and does not take much of your time.

Make sure that your e-mails are professional sounding and well written. If you send an e-mail full of abbreviations, misspellings, and poor grammar it will turn off your customers. They will think you are unprofessional and sloppy, and you will lose business. Write in a conversational, friendly style, but at the same time, make sure it is well written. Use your spell-checker. If you have a hard time composing a well-written sentence, do not do it yourself. Hire somebody else to do it for you. Sending a poorly-written e-mail is worse than sending no e-mail at all.

You will occasionally get an e-mail that sounds like an idiot wrote it, but treat all customers with respect, even if the question they are asking is unusual or obviously unnecessary. Suppose you list a cashmere scarf. Your heading reads, "Brand New Cashmere Scarf from India." You get the following e-mail:

"HAY THERE GOOD AUCTION WHATS THAT SCARV MADE OF AND IS IT USED? WHERE IT COME FROM???"

You would be surprised at how many e-mails like this you will receive from people who just do not read your listing very closely. Your first instinct is to ignore an e-mail like this, but ours is not to judge the intelligence level and literacy of our customers. The fact that your customer did not read your listing correctly and cannot write a coherent sentence does not mean that they are not going to buy what you have to offer. The fact that their questions could have been answered had they only read the heading of your listing is beside the point, and you do not need to point that out to them. Firing off an e-mail, "Read the listing. Your questions are answered there," may seem to make sense, but it is not going to make you any customers. Of course, they missed the information in the listing, did not read it, or just did not pay attention. Answer their e-mail promptly, politely, and address each of their questions. Make no mention of the fact that they should have just read your auction heading. Sign off by saying, "If you have any other questions, please feel free to contact me again." It is true that this customer may not be the sharpest knife in the drawer, but they have money to spend just like anybody else. A $5 bill in a Harvard graduate's pocket spends just the same as a $5 bill sitting in the pocket of an itinerant tobacco farmer with a third grade education.

A central tenet of good customer service is sticking to the old saw, "There are no stupid questions." True, there are questions that sound stupid to you, but the person asking them wants to know. Never make your customer feel unintelligent or stupid for asking the wrong question.

TIP: BUYER'S REMORSE

"Such buyers suffer from 'buyer's remorse,' but that is not considered an adequate reason for canceling a sale or giving a refund. eBay used to have an absolute policy that sales could not be cancelled by either the buyer or the seller, but they have loosened the policy up quite a bit for the sellers. Some sellers realize belatedly that they are selling their item too cheaply, and they can now cancel the sale even if there has been a bid on the auction, as long as there is 24 hours or more to go before the end of the auction.

-Arthur and Margo Lemner

"I Want My Money Back!"

There are plenty of eBay sellers who state prominently in their "About Me" page and on each listing, "All Sales Final!" This is an overly strict policy that will not win you any friends and will discourage some people from bidding at all. If a customer has never bought anything from you, remember that he does not know you at all. He has never met you, and he is considering buying a product based only on a description and photograph, not having actually seen it in person. You are just a page on the Internet, and he has all the reason in the world to be distrustful. Of course, you have no intention of doing so, but you have to communicate that to your bidders through friendly policies.

You will not get that many returns (unless you are selling substandard goods), so you do not have much to worry about. Every physical store in the world builds a certain number of returns into their pricing structure. It is inevitable that once in a great while, something may get broken in shipping, or when it arrives, it is not what the buyer expected. Instead of imposing a strict "No Returns" policy, create something a little friendlier. Create a return and refund policy stating that you will graciously accept returns within a set time, for example, 30 days. Be sure to state clearly in that policy how shipping fees will be handled, and what you expect your customer to do to facilitate the return and refund.

Payment Methods

A big part of customer service is just making things easier for your buyers. I have met eBay sellers who insist on being paid only by money order sent via U.S. mail. This policy will eliminate almost all of your business. The great attraction of buying something on eBay, or anywhere online, is that you do not have to leave your house. Your money order policy will force them to leave the house to go buy a money order and send it to you, thereby defeating the entire purpose of buying online in the first place. You must be willing to accept payment in as many different methods as possible to service your customer better and to attract more customers.

Of course, PayPal has become a de facto standard method of payment on eBay, so you should sign up for that. Most eBay buyers see it as very convenient. Also be willing to accept checks in the mail, since not everybody has or wants to have a PayPal account. Some customers may not use credit cards at all. If you do accept checks, it is reasonable to have a policy of waiting until the check clears before sending the goods, but the old standard of ten days' wait is obsolete. Because of a recent piece of federal legislation called "Check 21," banks now exchange paper checks electronically, and checks clear faster than they used to, very often the same day they are deposited. Check with your bank to find out more details.

Robert Sachs, RKS Solutions

Since I am selling on consignment, I spend a good deal of time working with my clients to ensure that they understand how eBay works, what I can and cannot do for them, and that the expected selling prices are acceptable. If they have a 'gotta have' price, I need to know that up front, before I even accept a product for sale. If their price is unrealistic, there's no need to try selling it on eBay—and I will then discuss options with them for using other sites or selling methods, lowering their price needs, or recommend they just donate the stock to a local charity.

"Some sellers incorrectly consider the cost of a good auction management toolset to be something they just cannot afford. But you have to compare the cost of the tools against the time saved. In my case, Blackthorne Pro saves me hours a day, time that I put to use doing other things that my software cannot do, like processing more inventory, taking images, packing, and shipping. A good software solution may take some time to set up, and it may seem like a great deal of work to get everything set up. However, the time saved can be used for many other things, even little things like attending a child's ballet recital or taking a family trip to the local park or zoo.

"My clients set their desired net price, and if I feel that price can be achieved, it is up to me to deliver it. I generally do NOT use nine-cent opening bids—in nearly every case where I have discussed it with a client, they have indicated they have no desire to sell anything at that price. We will then discuss a more realistic starting bid and desired selling price, and develop a strategy for their products based on those numbers and eBay sales history and fees. Failure to account for the eBay/PayPal fees can mean the difference between making and losing money—you have to consider **all** costs when determining price."

As with any business, return customers bring greater success and higher profits. The formula is simple. "Provide a great product at a fantastic price coupled with outstanding customer service and speedy delivery. Sounds corny, but it really is that simple. If the product is good enough to impress buyers, they will remember you and look you up when they want to buy again. If you provide the service and information they want, they will remember you as a helpful seller, interested in giving them the best for less. If it gets to them fast and in great condition (remember, that box is the first physical impression they have of your business—the rest has all been just talk), they will have fewer concerns about the speed and condition of future deliveries.

"You want your buyers to consider you the friendly local merchant who is interested in helping them, not the guy whispering from the dark alley about the 'great deal' you can make them tonight only."

Creating an environment where customers want to return is part of an overall growth strategy. "My goal is to always do better each year than the year before. That may be in the form of expanding product selection, increasing sales, and average selling price, or in lowering my cost of sales while maintaining sales and pricing. Each year brings new challenges and new opportunities. Addressing them successfully becomes a goal in itself sometimes.

"Growth will come from continued solid returns for my clients, continued selection for my customers, and continued service to both. Keeping my clients satisfied will keep the product coming. Keeping my customers satisfied will keep the sales growing."

Customer service as well forms a large part of that growth strategy. "Customer service should be 'reasonably personal'. It is unreasonable to think that any company is going to consider your one question or complaint before anything else, but it is quite reasonable to expect a company or seller to be polite, address your issues directly, and work to provide a mutually equitable solution. If buyers feel that you are aware of their concerns and will be working to deal with the situation, they will allow you the time to do so. When you can get positive feedback from a buyer who returned a product, you are handling your customer service well. When that same buyer returns and buys again, you are handling your customer service **very** well.

"I do use 'canned' messages, except for those questions that are answered in my listings and simply have not been read by the buyer. If a new question crops up and begins to show up repeatedly, I will address it in the listing template, in various e-mails (as appropriate), and perhaps even create a new canned message. All my e-mails reflect the same style I use when writing a direct response. One thing I have never cared for is cold canned replies. Blackthorne Pro allows me to answer most buyer questions (eBay mail) from within the software, which allows me to use a canned message to personalize it when needed. It means that I do not have to type and retype the same answers.

A Growth Strategy

There are two sure ways to fail in business: having no growth, and having uncontrolled growth. Every successful business has a growth plan. Growth does not just happen, and if you are unprepared for it, growth, if it happens too quickly, can actually kill your business.

But all growth should be good, right? Not necessarily. What would happen for example, to a business that had a marketing department that outpaced its production department? Orders come in for a million parts, but production can only generate half a million? All that new business would be lost.

There is a very big difference between an eBay business you work at part-time while holding a day job, and an eBay business that you work at full-time. You need different tools, different strategies, and a different approach.

How to Get There

The purpose of this chapter is really to look at how to prepare for growth; the rest of this book goes into how to achieve growth. It is two different fields. There are many ways to achieve growth, but when that growth comes, you have to be prepared. To summarize, here are a few ways that successful eBay entrepreneurs have achieved successful growth in their businesses:

1. Diversify your product line.

2. Advertise using pay-per-click ads from Google and eBay.

3. Keep a mailing list and send existing customers an informative newsletter.

4. Regularly review eBay auctions to see what is hot and what is not.

5. Expand your list of sources for unusual, high-margin products.

6. Create a Web site separate from eBay that is search-engine optimized and linked to your eBay site.

7. Set your business apart from others. Make it unique.

8. Keep inventory carrying costs to a minimum

When Do I Quit My Day Job?

Ah yes, that is the big question for any entrepreneur. The day job is a source of security, and we are all tempted to hang onto it. In my father's day, job security was prized very highly. After World War II, in my hometown of South Bend, Indiana, there were two great places to work: Bendix and Studebaker—good, union, blue-collar factory work. If you got into one of those places, you held onto the job for life and retired with a pension. Bendix and Studebaker were gods for people here. People trusted the founders and the companies. They believed in security, in hard work, and in being loyal to their employers. And while Bendix still exists after a fashion today, most of it is gone from South Bend. Studebaker went bankrupt, and people who had worked there for decades lost their pensions entirely.

The point of that story is not to put too much stock in job security. There is no such thing. It does not exist. No matter whom you work for and what promises they may have made you, they can disappear. If you have what is conventionally considered a "good job," many well-meaning people, especially friends and family, are going to tell you, "You better hang onto that job." What you must do is smile, nod, and ignore everything they say. You can provide yourself with just as much security as any employer can, no matter how large and apparently secure they may be. In fact, you can provide yourself with more, because you have direct control over your business.

One thing that an old Buddhist monk in a remote monastery described to me was "the impermanence of all things." Now this old fellow did not know what eBay was. He was not an entrepreneur and did not care much about money. But that wisdom permeates all life, all existence, and everything we do. Although that tenet comes from a spiritual foundation, its usefulness in practical, every day life is overwhelming. Despite the fact that Lord Buddha, who originally said it, was most decidedly not a businessman, that small phrase, when taken to heart, can even lead to success in business. You do not have to be a Buddhist, or even religious, to take this to heart and gain the advantage of this point of view.

When you think of your day job, you think of a company that gives you a paycheck regularly, and you tend to believe that your place of business will always be there. However, all things are impermanent. Corporate promises get broken, layoffs happen, and people get fired. Companies downsize or go out of business. What matters most to a company is their bottom line at the end of the quarter, and if the existence of your job becomes a deterrent to increasing that bottom line, you are out the door in a heartbeat. There is no such thing as job security. When you are able to lose the illusion of job security, you will no longer be dependent on that job. Instead of your job being your entire life, as it is for far too many people, your job becomes a thing that you do. You are not attached to it. You could just as easily be doing something else.

Quitting your day job, once you rid yourself of the illusion of job security, becomes a simple business decision. If you have reached the point in your eBay business when you are spending an inordinate amount of nights and weekends on it, you have perhaps hired a part-time assistant, your eBay income equals or exceeds the income from your day job, and you have plenty of money in the bank, it should be an easy decision to let go of the day job.

Keep Organized and Use Lots of Software

When you first start out, and you have ten or so auctions up at a time, you can easily keep track of everything with a set of index cards and a pencil. But if you are managing a hundred auctions at a time, you will quickly get behind with that sort of strategy. You will lose orders and you will disservice customers. Think back to that day job you used to have (or still have). Chances are your employer used automation to advantage. All employers do. It is how they save money. I remember working in an office in the early days of desktop computers. There was a monthly business spreadsheet that was being done, and it took three clerks five days of manual labor to prepare it. I took the project over, put it in a spreadsheet program, and did the whole thing in a couple of hours. The employees who had previously been in charge of it were a little ticked off at me for showing them up, but eventually they went onto other things, and the company was a little bit more efficient for everyone.

It is best to try to stay at least a little bit ahead of the curve and have access to plenty of good tools, computers, and software. Of course, there is no need for overkill, and you do not need a supercomputer, but you will need a good, powerful desktop computer with broadband Internet access. Do not try to do it with dial-up. You will waste too much time and tie up your phone. You will also need a full set of productivity applications including a spreadsheet, a word processor, and an HTML editor/Web design package. Other optional but very useful software tools include a small business accounting package and e-mail list management software.

Once your business starts to grow, you will spend an inordinate amount of time on fulfillment. It will be easy to lose track of your overall strategy simply by getting bogged down with spending all your time putting things in boxes and going to the post office. The more time you spend on those routine tasks, the less time you will have for more important things, like finding new things to sell, creating attractive listings, and designing ad campaigns. A postal scale and postage printer will also save you time. Once your business gets going, you will be surprised at how much time you waste going to the post office and standing in line to buy postage. Get a postal printer that you can load with funds ahead of time, so you can weigh your packages and print out postage at home. Get an account with UPS as well, and arrange for home pickup. That alone could save you hours a week.

Do Not Be Attached To One Category

Earlier, I talked about how to apply the philosophy of "all things are impermanent" to your day job. The same philosophy must be applied to your eBay business itself.

That is not to say that your eBay business will not last long, but the nature of it will be very transitory. You may well find that one type of item sells quite well for several months, but the market may switch very quickly. A Western philosopher may say, "Do not be a one-trick pony." The result is the same. Many eBay sellers simply think small. They latch onto one very small category of product and build a business around it to the exclusion of any other product category. It may work well, because that niche product is hot, but it will not last. You will make money for a while. Then the product will go through its natural cycle, and you will be left with nothing.

Experiment with multiple products and multiple categories. When you start a new one, do not invest too much into it right away until you see how well it is going to sell. Never make assumptions that a particular item is going to be popular, just because you think it will. Some product categories just will not make it. But you will not know until you give it a try. If you just have a one-product category, you will make some sales for a while, but if you offer ten-product categories, and five of them sell well, you have a flourishing, growing business. Forget about the five that did not sell well, cut your losses, and give them away as Christmas presents. You still have five left that are bringing in plenty of money, and you are making five times as much as you would if you would have just stuck with the single product category.

A large part of growing a business is not being afraid to try new things.

Hiring Staff

The vast majority of eBay entrepreneurs work solo, but your ambition is that your business grows larger. If your ambitions are realized, you will need employees. Having even a part-time person to help out on the fulfillment end, which is probably by far the most time-consuming and most tedious, can free up your time for more important things. While you are focusing on finding great new products and creating attention-getting listings, your part-time staff can be stuffing the boxes, keeping the books, or answering your e-mails for you.

Even if you are only hiring a part-time person to work out of your home office, you are still moving into a completely new category. You are becoming an employer, and there are obligations and responsibilities that you will have. It may all seem very informal to you, but you still have to follow the rules, such as no cash under the table. That may be great for the employee, but it is not going to help you. Pay your employee with a check, withhold all the appropriate payroll taxes, and file them with the various taxing agencies. It is only by doing that that you will be able to deduct your staff's wages from your own taxes.

If you are like most eBay sellers, you work out of a home office. When hiring, make it clear at the outset, either in the ad or when they call you on the phone, that they will be working in a home office. The reason for that is clear. Not everyone is comfortable working in somebody's home, and you will weed out those who object right off the bat. On the subject of the home office, there is a difference between a home office where you work solo and a home office where you have staff. I, for one, work solo. My home office is not particularly neat, and there are stacks of papers sitting around on the floor at this moment. I have five projects going, and there are five stacks of papers and folders. My wife is out of town taking care of her father as I am writing this, and there are six coffee cups sitting on my desk. My trash can is overflowing. I am working on installing floor tile, and there is a bucket of cement sitting next to my computer. That is all well and good if it is just you there. But when you start bringing in employees, you have to keep your office a bit neater, a bit more organized, and a bit more professional. Of course, it is your home, and it will always look like a home, but it also has to look somewhat like a workplace.

Chicshades

If you have ever bought a pair of cool sunglasses from eBay, chances are you got it from Steven at Chicshades, a small eBay business that sells celebrity and designer-inspired sunglasses. Although he has only been selling on eBay under this ID for less than a year, he has been active since 2003. Currently, he manages between 40 and 80 listings for every three to five day period. Although he still holds down a day job, his eBay business continues to grow, and he looks forward to increasing his volume to 100 to 150 items per week. He has a strong and successful growth strategy. His initial goal was to make Powerseller status, a goal that he achieved within three months. "My next goal is to climb up to Silver Powerseller status, but keep my profit margin at the same level and keep my 100 percent feedback rating." His growth strategy also includes adding additional product lines.

Steven does not limit his activity to eBay. He also maintains his own e-commerce Web site, **www.celebrityglasses.com**. While he also has sold on other auction venues, including **iOffer.com**, **Overstock.com**, and **Amazon.com**, he said, "eBay seems to have the best turnaround for my products." Having his own Web site in addition to eBay, however, has been an excellent move. **www. Celebrityglasses.com** is an attractive and professional-looking site with plenty of pictures of celebrities wearing great-looking sunglasses. Who can resist a sunglasses site with a picture of the Blues Brothers on the front? Steven is not leaving his business's future in the hands of eBay exclusively. "My eBay business currently represents about 90 percent of my business, but I plan to change that around soon, since my profit margin/potential is much greater on my e-commerce site."

Steven had some good advice about making a small eBay business into a large one, and he has done quite well in that regard already. "The best advice," he said, "is to start out small and build up your volume at a slow and steady pace. If things get out of hand by having too much volume, you might put yourself in a tricky situation by not being able to fulfill orders and answer e-mails. You also need to learn how to scale your business by using the right set of online selling tools that are available. There are many great eBay books on the market, but I have found the best resources are found by joining an eBay group in your local area. I also heard from other eBay members that 'eBay LIVE' is a great resource for sellers wanting to make their eBay businesses larger. The eBay message boards are a huge resource and have been a great benefit for me."

CHAPTER 24

Nickels and Dimes

Even a big business can be "nickeled and dimed" to death, and so it is with your eBay business. There are endless expenses and fees. If you do not keep track of these little nuisances, your business could very well be in danger.

The fact is, many of these expenses are minor. When you are running a small business, you have a tendency to overlook minor expenses, but in the end, they add up, and can easily eat up all of your profits before too long.

Major Cost Centers

In business, we speak of profit centers and cost centers. These terms are self-explanatory. Certain functions are done to generate profit directly. Others support the overall business, indirectly generating profit and their main purpose is spending the company's money. Cost centers can be found in unusual places and can become a problem. It is essential to keep track of them and minimize those costs whenever possible.

In an eBay business, the three biggest common cost centers are:

- eBay listing fees

- Packing and shipping material

- Staff (for larger eBay businesses)

- Storage/office space

I will not include the actual cost of the goods you are selling here. That would fall more in the category of "cost of goods sold," and is more of a direct profit-generating expense rather than a mere cost center. There are, of course, countless other minor cost centers, including office supplies, software (it is very easy to get addicted to buying more and more business software!), and legal/accounting services. Each one must be regulated closely. Hiring an accounting service is a great convenience, but if your business is still small, you could easily spend your entire profit on an accountant. Do the books yourself until your business has grown large enough to merit outsourcing the function.

There is, of course, a fundamental difference between a small business and a large one, and that is the concept of do-it-yourself. As a small business owner, you will need to start out doing your own accounting, filing some of your own legal/organizational papers, running your own errands, and serving as everything from floor sweeper to CEO. There is a natural temptation to want to outsource these jobs immediately, but you must resist that temptation. Outsourcing these functions too early in your small business will result in a much longer period before you are profitable. If you are like most small businesspersons, you do not have bags of money on hand to subsidize an unprofitable business for very long.

Robert Sachs, RKS Solutions

Of course, a common complaint—particularly as competition grows on eBay—is that profit margins are decreasing. Nonetheless, profit is still possible.

Bob's advice: "One of the consultants whose e-mails I read regularly has a saying—'you make your profit when you buy, not when you sell.'

"His example: If you buy $10 bills for $5 and sell them on eBay for $10, where do you make your money? You make your profit by knowing a good deal when you see it and buying those $10 bills for $5 each. You collect that profit when you sell the bills.

"If you are paying attention to your market on eBay, know your products, and consider **all** your costs when making that profit/no profit calculation. You should be able to make money on every eBay sale. This does not mean you will make a ton of money on every sale. Just that you should be able to cover your expenses, your replacement costs, and have a bit extra to show for it.

"The better deal you get when you purchase, the more profit you recoup when you sell. But you won't make any profit if you do not know your product, know its performance on eBay, and make your purchase correctly."

eBay Listing Fees

One of the loudest complaints of eBay sellers is the eBay listing fees. There are a great many different things you can spend money on with eBay, and the listing fees can rapidly consume a large share of your profits if you are not careful.

The easiest way to fail on eBay is to list absolutely everything and anything you have without paying attention to whether you think it will sell. It is easy to think, "Well, if it doesn't sell, I've only lost the listing fee." But when you multiply that $1 or $2 times hundreds of items, you have spent a significant amount of money to list things that are not selling.

Suppose your average listing fee is $1 per item. One dollar does not sound like much to risk, but in reality, it is more than $1 if you are not selling every single thing you list, and most people do not. If you list a hundred items and sell five of them, you have not really spent $1 per item. You have spent $20 per item. The most important ratio here is not the amount of listing fees per item listed, but the amount of listing fees divided by the items that have been sold.

You do not need to do the full treatment for every single item. There are extra cents to be paid for every bold listing, every extra photo, and every special placement. Use those extra eBay features sparingly. If you have a high dollar item likely to attract attention, spend the extra money to get the prominent listings, but it is wasteful to take that approach with every single item you have.

There are many options you can take advantage of on your eBay listings, but unfortunately, almost all of them cost extra money. The basic auction listing is reasonably priced, but limited. On the other hand, if you add too many of the extra options, your listing fees can eat up your profits.

When you do decide to take advantage of some of the extra listing options, you can save a little money by looking at the price breakdown. Fee prices are usually set based on price range. There may be a big difference in your eBay fees, for example, between an item being sold at $19.99 and an item being sold at $2. Pricing your items accordingly can save you money in listing fees.

Packing and Shipping Material

The price for packing material and boxes varies a great deal. If you buy your boxes and packing material (bubble wrap, packing peanuts) at the local drugstore, you are likely to be paying at least ten times what you should be paying for it. You can easily go down to your local drugstore or supermarket and spend $4 or $5 just to buy a single box, and enough bubble wrap and filler material to send a single package. Are you even making $5 on average for each item you sell? Many people are not. Sure, local department stores and drugstores have these items, and it is very convenient for people who have only one or two things to ship, but you are running a business. You need to buy these items in large quantities from large office supply stores or specialty suppliers.

How much does it cost to ship a package, not including postage? Many eBay sellers do not even keep track of things like this, but you must. Some of the biggest dotcom failures of the recent boom collapsed precisely for this reason: their fulfillment costs exceeded their profits. Shipping materials will be one of your largest expenses, so it is worthwhile to devote some time to compare prices for boxes, bubble wrap, and filler material at your local office supply stores. They are where you will find the best deals locally. There are also some eBay sellers who specialize in selling these sorts of materials to other eBay sellers, so check on eBay directly as well. With very little effort, it will be possible to cut your fulfillment costs.

Staff

If your growth ambitions are realized, you will need to hire some staff at some point. As with any expenditure, avoid hiring staff prematurely, because this can be a very major expense. eBay, as with many businesses, may be cyclical. There will be downtimes and uptimes. There will be times of the year when you have more business than you can handle, but there will also be times when it is slow. This is a natural cycle of any sort of business, especially in direct sales. However, employees tend to expect regular hours. You have a dilemma. Ideally, you would like to have an employee who would come in whenever you need them and leave when the work is done. There is nothing more frustrating to an employer than seeing an employee with nothing to do. But for most employees, the ideal is the exact opposite—regular hours, same time every week, same number of hours. I hope that you can find a happy medium that satisfies both parties.

It is likely that at least at first, you will be content with part-time staff. Very few eBay sellers actually have full-time employees, although there may come a time when it becomes necessary for you. Until that day, however, part-timers with flexible needs are best. The best scenario is to find someone like a student or housewife/househusband who just wants extra spending money and is not dependent on a paycheck to pay bills. With such an individual, you not need feel guilty when the work is slow and you do not need them to come in.

There will be seasonal times—like around Christmas—when you are doing more business, and may even need to have a full-time person, but only temporarily. You can often find people wanting full-time temporary work at universities. A student on winter break would be ideal for helping you out with the Christmas rush.

Of course, do not overlook the possibility of using "casual labor" from your spouse or kids who are much more likely to work for you just to help out and get a little extra spending money on an irregular basis. If you do employ family members, however, do not pay them "under the table," or you will risk losing track of your payroll expenses entirely and letting it go out of control. Even your own children should be paid with a legitimate paycheck with taxes withheld, so you can have an audit trail and can legitimately deduct that expense from your own taxes.

Storage/Office Space

You will probably start out working out of your home. If you have a spare room that you can dedicate solely to your eBay business, so much the better. There are two advantages to this strategy. First, it is just easier to stay organized if you are not running your eBay business off your kitchen table, and you have some dedicated space for it. Second, you can probably qualify for the home office deduction, which will save you some money on your taxes.

But there are circumstances where the home office will not work. Maybe you just do not have the space. Rather than renting an office space before your business can support it, the best strategy is just to hold off for as long as you can and try your best to keep your space organized. Get the outside office space as soon as you can, but do not do it prematurely.

If the biggest problem is storing goods, you may consider just renting a storage space instead of office space, which is likely to be much cheaper.

If you do find that renting an office is absolutely necessary, you can still cut costs there by sharing space or perhaps subletting part of an office from another company. It is common for larger companies to have rooms they are not using and are willing to sublet. Alternately, if you are enterprising and interested in real estate (read my other book: *The Part-Time Real Estate Investor: How to Generate Huge Profits While Keeping Your Day Job*), you may consider buying an inexpensive but large house, and converting it to office space, taking the space you need and renting out the rest to cover your payments. Ideally, you would break even or maybe make a small profit on the deal.

Arthur and Margo Lemner

eBay sellers have to be very sensitive to the profit margin, especially as the field heats up and more sellers enter the market. Profit margins naturally decrease as a result. Margo notes, "The profit margin depends on how valuable your items are. If they are inexpensive, you may spend a great deal of time making very little money. We have learned to avoid selling items that are too recent or too plentiful to be worth much to a collector. Also, if items do not sell after a second auction period, we usually withdraw them to avoid having the listing fees eat up all the profits. If you are selling regularly, you know what the various fees will add up to, including the PayPal fee for receiving the payment.

"We determine prices partly based on our own knowledge of the quality, age, condition, and attractiveness of the item. The best source of pricing information is eBay itself. We check what similar items have sold for or not sold for in completed auctions. eBay used to make that information available for the month following the close of the auction in advanced searches. Now the period is only two weeks, which can make it more difficult to find a price for items that are relatively rare. This can be time consuming, however, because sometimes you have to read each auction description to know if the item is equivalent to the one you want to sell. We also use eBay pricing research to sell items on eBay and also to buy items from eBay."

Selling Individual Items Versus Bulk

Selling unique items is the basis of many successful eBay businesses, but this takes work since you must create individual listings for every item. Another strategy is to find a good item that you can buy many of and sell the same item with consecutive, identical listings or a "Dutch Auction."

There are obvious advantages to each strategy. For many, the very nature of eBay is that it is a venue for selling unique collectible items, and so those types of eBay businesses are built not around buying and selling multiples of identical goods, but unique goods in a certain category. That is more the traditional eBay model that everybody knows and loves.

Even if you do sell unique collectibles, there may be occasions when you come across a great deal on multiple copies of a certain item. You can build your entire business around this type of bulk model. The advantages to selling multiples of the same item are obvious. You are able to gain leverage through purchasing power since you are buying several of the same item instead of one. You get a better price break, and theoretically at least, your profit margin will be greater.

If you do come across several identical items that you need to sell, you do have some alternatives. Suppose you get a deal on a dozen of something. You can set up a dozen separate auctions and sell them individually. But unless the item is something that you are pretty sure will sell out, you could lose money in listing fees if you do not sell them all, and this approach is often impractical. Also if you have more than ten, eBay will not let you list them all individually at the same time. You could sell all ten of them as a single lot; however, this is often impractical because most buyers do not want that many of what you have to offer. The last remaining option is the Dutch auction, which is described in the section below.

Buying From Wholesalers

Many successful eBay entrepreneurs have unique items on offer that they have collected at yard sales, estate sales, and other sources. Not everybody follows that model, and you do not have to. You can also obtain great items to re-sell from wholesalers; but the only difference there is that when you buy from a wholesaler, you are not just buying one item.

Logistically, it is a very different business model. When you are out scouring the countryside for unique antiques and collectibles, you are buying one thing at a time and evaluating each item for its salability. If you go out for a weekend and buy a hundred different collectibles, it will not matter that much if you overestimate the value of just one of them. On the other hand, if you go out and buy a wholesale lot of a hundred of just one item, you need to be reasonably certain ahead of time that you have made a good deal, that what you have will sell out, and that you can turn a profit on it. If you are dealing in large lots, one mistake can cost you a fortune.

When you are buying lots of individual items, you can take a risk on one item if you are not completely sure about its salability, but that risk takes on greater proportions when you buy in bulk. Buy on this basis only if you are very familiar with the market.

If you do embark on this strategy, however, there are plenty of great places where you can buy items at tremendous discounts, and you will get deals that you would not be able to get if you are trying to buy just singles of different items. If you are going to deal in basic commodity items for example, like laptop computers, printers, or other electronics, you may be better off buying in wholesale lots and selling with Dutch auctions.

If you buy a large lot of something on a wholesale basis, you may not sell out of them with a single Dutch auction, but this does not have to be a disaster.

The Dutch auction can be used as your first sales path, but there is no reason that you cannot have multiple sales paths. Sell as many as can be sold through the Dutch auction because that is where you will sell the most in the shortest amount of time. After that, see how many you have left, and you can sell them through individual eBay auctions, in your eBay store, or through your other non-eBay electronic storefront.

The Dutch Auction

There is a different type of auction format you use when you are selling more than one of the same item, and it is called a Dutch auction. Why it is called a "Dutch" auction is a mystery. I suspect it is rather like French fries, which are not really French. We do attribute many things incorrectly to other countries, like pizza, which is not Italian, and chop suey, which is not native to China. When two people split the bill, we call it "going Dutch," although I am pretty sure people in Holland do not do that any more than in any other country. In fact, I was surprised to discover that in Thailand, splitting the bill according to each person's order is called dining "American style." Nonetheless, with apologies to any of my readers from Holland, I will follow convention and refer to these unusual auctions as "Dutch auctions."

It sounds simple. A Dutch auction occurs when you are selling two or more of the same item in the same auction. However, it gets more complicated than that. Here is how it works: You set a minimum bid price. Bidders say how many of the item they would like and the highest price per item they are willing to pay. Upon close of the auction, the lowest successful bid (that is, the bid that is closest to, but not under, your minimum bid price) wins, and all bidders pay that amount.

To make it a Dutch auction, you do have to have multiples of the same item, and they have to be exactly identical. It would not be fair if everybody is paying the same amount of money, but the items are even slightly different. If you get in a shipment of a dozen laptops, for example, and they are similar, but not quite the same — some may have more RAM and some may have more hard disk space — then you cannot sell them with a Dutch auction. They have to be all identical.

Here is an example. Suppose you have ten identical DVD players. You got a deal. Your cost was $20 each, and so you figure a minimum sale price of $35 would cover your cost, listing fees and other expenses, and a reasonable profit margin. You set your minimum bid for $35. Then the bids start to come in. A few people bid under that $35 bid price, but you get some other good bids. A handful of people bid $40, a few more bid $45 and one bids $50. At the last minute, one bid comes in at $35. When your auction closes, you discover that you have nine bids that are either at or above your $35 minimum bid. You then sell the DVDs to all nine bidders for the price of $35 each, even if they bid more than that.

When setting your minimum bid in a Dutch auction, you must realize that in reality, you are not likely to sell your items for much more than your minimum bid. Because of the nature of the auction, the lowest acceptable bid that comes in is quite likely to be at or near your minimum, and Dutch auctions tend to gravitate to that lowest acceptable price. So when you set that minimum, set it realistically, because that is probably the amount you will receive.

Now suppose, however, that you have 15 bids that come in at $35 or more. You have only ten products, though. In this case, you take the tenth highest bid, and set the price according to that bid. You sell the products to the ten highest bidders. The other five, even if they bid at $35 or more, do not get to buy.

If you are selling multiples of the same item, the Dutch auction option is often the best avenue, if for no other reason, it saves you money in listing fees. It is easy to set one up. Just start a regular auction listing, enter in a quantity greater than one in the "quantity" field, and eBay will automatically assign your auction as a "Dutch" auction.

Auctions Versus "Buy It Now," Fixed-Price Listings, and Other Alternatives

In the last chapter, we looked at the "Dutch Auction" alternative. By far, the most frequently used format is the standard auction format, where you list an item, and people bid on it. The Dutch Auction presents another method, where you have multiple identical items, and list them in a single auction. If you have ten items, then the top ten bidders win, and each of those top ten bidders pay the same amount of money, which is the tenth-highest bid.

But the Dutch version is not the only alternative to the standard straight auction.

As eBay grows in size and you get more and more competition each day, you must look to alternatives to keep your business strong. In the early days of eBay, the standard auction was a strong method of selling, and you could make money very easily, often selling items for even more than their value. But as eBay has grown in popularity, two things have happened. Buyers have gotten savvier, and more sellers are in on the act.

Buyers now see eBay as a way to find good, unusual items at a discounted price, often at far less than they would have to pay if they were to buy the same thing at a local brick-and-mortar shop. Your profit margins are going to be slimmer. You have more competition as well. More sellers are selling the same sorts of things, or in many cases, exactly the same thing, as you. That gives buyers more choice, and that naturally tends to bring down the price on all items on offer. As a result, sellers who rely exclusively on a standard auction format are at a disadvantage.

"Buy It Now"

Auctions can be fun, but sometimes when you are shopping, you want something now and do not want to wait. The downside of the auction is that people can lose interest over the duration of the auction, or they may just be in a hurry to get something and are not interested in waiting out the auction before they get their item.

That is why eBay added the "Buy It Now" option. With this option, the buyer does not have to wait until the end of the auction to get the item. Your item is displayed as a regular auction item and listed with all the other regular auctions, but just includes "Buy It Now" as an option. If a buyer takes advantage of this option, then the auction ends. The "Buy It Now" button appears on your listing, but remains only until someone makes a bid on the item, and then the "Buy It Now" button disappears. The option is not available for Dutch auctions.

As with everything on eBay, almost all options cost extra money, and so it is with "Buy It Now." To add this option, you will have to pay an extra fee, from between five cents and twenty five cents.

Setting your "Buy It Now" price requires a little thought. You will probably want to set this price above your starting bid price, but still not too high. If you set the "Buy It Now" price too high, not only will you not get any "Buy It Now" customers, but you may also scare off bidders for the standard auction. Even though bidders are not obligated in any way to bid your "Buy It Now" price, the psychological effect of seeing a price that they consider to be too high will cause them to lose interest.

Fixed Price Listings

The "Fixed Price" option differs a little from the "Buy It Now" option. "Buy It Now" allows you to set a fixed price, but offers some limitations. While "Buy It Now" allows you to take advantage of the standard auction format while also allowing an immediate purchase, the "Buy It Now" option will disappear when the bidding starts.

The "Fixed Price" option offers a slightly different approach, allowing you to bypass the standard auction format entirely, and simply list an item for sale at a fixed price, just like any other retail store. The transaction is immediate. Buyers do not have to wait for an auction to end.

This option will also manifest itself with the "Buy It Now" button, but unlike a straight "Buy It Now" transaction, "Fixed Price" does not include the auction option, and your listing will not show a "Place Bid" button.

"Fixed Price" listings also differ a little from simply adding the "Buy It Now" option to an auction. To offer a "Fixed Price" item, you have to be established as an eBay seller with a feedback rating of at least 30.

To sell an item with a "Fixed Price" option, just click the "Fixed Price" option on the Sell page, where it says, "How would you like to sell your item?"

Reserve Price

Some eBay sellers who stick with the standard, basic format occasionally are disappointed when their item sells for less than they wanted. Some beginners stick with the most basic listing, with no options to save money on listing fees. While saving money on listing fees is a solid strategy, and you definitely can go overboard with the listing extras, this strategy can end up costing you more than you saved on the listing fees.

The "Reserve Price" option of course costs extra money, but you may want to consider it. Many sellers have gone on eBay thinking that they would get big money for their items, then have been very disappointed to receive only small bids, and then end up losing money when they are obligated to send out items for less than what they paid for them.

Now if you are just clearing out your attic, that may be all well and good, since anything you get is clear profit. But if you are trying to make it a business, you are not going to last very long selling everything on a "no minimum" basic auction format. Buyers are savvy, and there is a hot competition so that if you list in this way, you stand a very good chance of becoming obligated to sell that $100 item for $1.

To protect themselves, many eBay sellers set a "Reserve Price." This price is hidden from the bidders. It is the lowest price you are willing to accept. If somebody places a bid that is lower than the reserve, you are not obligated to accept it.

While you do want to set a reserve price adequate enough to protect you from losses, keep in mind too that this is just the lowest acceptable bid, and the bidding will increase from there. Setting a reserve price that is too high will discourage bidding.

If you have taken advantage of this option, until such time as the reserve is met, your auction page will show to bidders the caption "Reserve Not Met." This tells all bidders that the minimum acceptable bid has not yet been placed.

At the end of the auction, if the reserve price still has not been met, you are not obligated to sell the item to anyone. Of course you do have the option to do so. For example, if the highest bidder is only $1 below your reserve, you may wish to go ahead and offer the item to that individual.

Second Chance Offer

Yes, it happens sometimes that your winning bidder does not come through for you. Who knows why? Maybe they had an unexpected expense, they cannot come up with the money, or maybe they are just flaky. More often than not, they do not even bother to get in touch with you to let you know they cannot fulfill their part of the deal. Now when that happens, you can block them from future bidding and even give them negative feedback, but none of those actions will make you any money.

What do you do when you are left holding the bag after an auction? You have had several bids on your item, but the winner is nowhere to be found. The "Second Chance Offer" option lets you offer your item to bidders who did not win but are the next highest under the winning bidder. If your winner backs out, you can offer the item to the one who came in second.

Another creative use of the "Second Chance Offer" allows you to sell multiples of an item without having to do a Dutch auction. You can offer the same product (assuming you have enough of them to go around) to any or all bidders who underbid, at the price they bid. The underbidders will receive a "Second Chance Offer" e-mail form you, with a link to a fixed price listing that is visible only to that bidder, and only for a limited amount of time that you set.

There are advantages to using this strategy. First of all, if you have multiple items, you can sell several of them through a single auction, and you can decide the cutoff point below which you will not accept the price. Unlike the Dutch auction, where you sell multiple items all at an identical price, the "Second Chance" auction option lets you sell multiples at different prices, based on each person's final bid price. Ultimately, you stand a chance of making more money selling multiples this way than through a Dutch auction.

Also, this method is a little more secretive than the Dutch auction. It is part of a standard auction. Bidders do not know that you plan to offer the "Second Chance." Also, bidders do not know how many of each item you have, while in the Dutch auction they see on the listing page the quantity of the item you possess.

A great advantage here too is that it does not cost you any more in listing fees. You can sell several of an item from just a single listing! And because you are planning to sell multiple items from a single listing, you may feel freer to take advantage of eBay's special listing options that give your listing greater prominence, since the total listing fee is in reality spread across multiple items you are selling, instead of just one.

Private Auction

There are few circumstances where you would find a private auction useful, but there are a few. In a private auction, all bidders are anonymous. Typically, in other auction formats, any seller can see the User IDs of all other bidders. In the private auction, you as the seller can see the identities of the bidders, but nobody else can. In most cases, it does not make that much difference who is bidding against you as a buyer, but in some rare occasions, if you are auctioning off a high-value item and you may be getting some well-known bidders, you may wish to impose the private auction option to protect their privacy. Another reason to use a private auction is if you are selling something sensitive or adult in nature.

Live Auctions

If you have ever been to a live auction, you know that it can be exciting. You are sitting in the audience and seeing the bidding going on around you, and you have to think fast. eBay is different from that, and the online auction format gives you the opportunity to think out your strategy at a more leisurely pace.

On some rare occasions, however, you may wish to hold a live auction on eBay, and eBay gives you the opportunity to do so. Usually the live auctions are for special auction events or very rare or unusual items, and you will not want to use this option for your day-to-day items that you sell on a regular basis. You can find out more about eBay's live auction option at **http://www.eBayliveauctions.com**. Most sellers offering goods in this manner are established auction houses.

Arthur and Margo Lemner

Promotion is different for every eBay seller, and since Art and Margo deal primarily with one-of-a-kind items, Margo said, "The best promotion is to have a good description and photos on each auction page and to make sure the items are competitively priced and in the correct eBay categories. In the process of checking other eBay auctions to find out what the going rate was for equivalent items, we occasionally found buyers bidding high for the same item we wanted to sell. In this case, we could e-mail the non-winning bidders to let them know we had another of the items available. This type of activity has to be judiciously used, because eBay does not allow SPAM. The banner ads cost more so that they are only appropriate for items that should sell very high."

How Do They Know You Are Legit?

Consumer awareness of fraud is at an all-time high, and there is some natural reluctance to make a purchase from an unknown seller. You can assuage that fear with tools like online escrow or bonding guarantees.

PayPal Buyer Protection

Being able to display the "PayPal Protection" icon on your Web page will also enhance your credibility a great deal. Showing this icon and being part of that program will offer your buyers a little bit more reassurance that you are legit, and they are going to get what they expect to get.

PayPal Protection is a program that offers up to $1,000 in protection for items that are not received. You have to have a PayPal business or premier account to offer this protection, and you also have to have at least 50 feedback comments and a 98 percent positive rating. And the great thing about this program is that it is free!

Escrow Services

If you are selling high dollar items, buyers have even more reason to be cautious and mistrusting of you, or anybody else for that matter. Usually, when you are selling ordinary, low-value items for $5 or $10, you receive payment first, and then ship out the item. But suppose you are selling something for $1,000. The buyer does not want to send you the money without getting the item in hand first, but you as seller, do not want to send out the item without receiving payment first. Escrow services provide a handy way to overcome this mutual distrust.

Both parties deal through the escrow agent. You send the item to the escrow agent, not the customer. The customer sends payment to the escrow agent, not you. The escrow agent, once satisfied that both parties have met their obligations, will then make the transfer. The buyer will have an agreed-upon amount of time to inspect the item before payment is transferred from the escrow agent to the seller.

Of course, even the escrow service can be crooked, so you need to find one that is reputable and has an established name, such as www.**Escrow.com**, which is approved by eBay. Naturally, there is an extra fee involved, which may be anywhere up to 3 percent of the sale price. It is up to you and the buyer to decide who pays the escrow fee. You may decide to cover the cost or agree to split the cost, although some sellers insist that the buyer bear the entire cost.

There have been some fraudulent operators who pretend to be escrow services. Proceed with caution. If you have never heard of the escrow service before, do some investigating before using their services, or just stick with the ones that have an established reputation.

Bonding Guarantees

This is another type of guarantee that offers reassurance to sellers, and also is useful for those who are dealing in high-value items. Like escrow services, it is not really worth the extra expense if you are dealing in $10 or $20 goods.

Bonding is a type of insurance policy. It provides a guarantee to the buyer, that if the seller does not fulfill his or her obligation, the bonding agency will satisfy that obligation one way or another, usually with a refund. One such reputable bonding guarantee service is BuySAFE, **www.buysafe.com**, which is often used for eBay transactions.

To offer bonding guarantees, you apply with the bonding agency. They evaluate your application and do various background checks on you. You pay a fee, and then display the logo from the bonding agent on your Web site. The BuySAFE logo is common, and many buyers will recognize it, giving them a greater level of confidence in your online store.

Buyers do not have to pay a fee to enjoy the protection of the bonding agent. You, as seller, pay a fee that is equal to a percentage of the transaction, usually about one percent. The fee applies only when goods are actually sold; if an auction item goes unsold, then you do not have to pay. You can also decide to apply the protection either to all your auctions or only to select auctions. Many sellers decide to use the bonding guarantee only for higher-value auctions.

Square Trade

Another common logo is the "Square Trade" logo, which is another tool that helps to create confidence. Square Trade is not part of eBay but is recommended by eBay. It is simply a dispute resolution agency that helps in case a seller and buyer have a disagreement. There is a $20 fee for resolution services. Even if the fee wipes out your profits, it may still be worthwhile to pay it because if the dispute is resolved amicably, you may be able to have negative feedback removed. That is worth much more than $20. Too much negative feedback can kill an eBay business very quickly.

You may be able to qualify to display the SquareTrade "seal of approval." Displaying the logo on your auction pages will create confidence. Of course, if you are a holder of the SquareTrade seal, SquareTrade checks your feedback and reports periodically to make sure you continue to be a legitimate seller. They will take back their seal if they suspect foul play. Buyers know this, of course, and so displaying the seal is of great value.

Arthur and Margo Lemner

"We regularly get scam e-mails telling us that there is a problem with an auction we have on eBay. These are what eBay calls 'spoofs,' which is a rather innocuous name for a crook trying to rob you. They want to get you to click on the links provided in the e-mail and input your eBay ID and password. Once they have that, they immediately put up attractive sounding auctions on eBay in your name, making use of your good feedback rating to get buyers to send their payments to the scammers. The buyers never receive their items, and they think you are to blame. eBay wants all such e-mails forwarded to **spoof@eBay.com** and then deleted. eBay also has information on their site to help people learn to spot the spoofs. eBay NEVER asks you to input your ID or password in an e-mail. There is also an Internet fraud site to contact if you cannot get satisfaction from eBay or PayPal."

Auction Management Tools

For a small-time seller moving a handful of items, it is easy to keep track of things manually, but if you are approaching this as a business, you will soon grow beyond that. Just keeping all of your listings up to date can quickly become a full-time job for a Powerseller, and you may wish to consider looking at some of the automated auction management tools, such as eBay's own Turbo Lister.

You will not need many of these tools immediately, but over time you will find them useful. As your business grows, you must make effective use of your time. There will be more to do as your business grows, and automation can be a wonderful thing. I have met people who spend an inordinate amount of time creating and managing a listing for an item that they will sell for a profit of only a few dollars. It just does not make sense to do that. Your time would be better spent working a minimum wage job. But with the right amount of computers and automation, much of that work can be eliminated or minimized, and you can manage hundreds of listings in the same amount of time it takes you to manage just a few.

There are some common tools that eBay sellers like to use, but software is software, and there are always new ones appearing. Do not be afraid to look around and choose the one that works best for you. If you are particularly adept at spreadsheets, you can do some of the work with an Excel spreadsheet and a few simple macro commands and save yourself the money you would spend buying specialized software tools.

Tools from eBay

eBay itself does not miss a beat, and they have made the big money by providing everything a seller and buyer needs and charging for it at every step. Many of the tools available from eBay are excellent and widely used. Since most other eBay sellers use them, you have a ready-made support group. These eBay seller tools are usually quite affordable when compared with other special-use software tools, and some are even free like the Turbo Lister.

- **Turbo Lister.** If you have only a handful of items, Turbo Lister will not be particularly useful, but once you get into higher volumes, it is great. It is used for creating multiple listings and can even be used with other software tools. Besides saving time, Turbo Lister also helps you to add an element of uniformity and professionalism to your listings. The way it works is that you are able to create your auction listings offline — this in itself saves time — and then you log on, and Turbo Lister posts all of the listings automatically for you. Turbo Lister provides you with several different themes, layouts, and prebuilt templates. The eBay templates cost time if you use them in a listing, but you can create your own templates, add them to the HTML view, and use them for free. You can see your listings in HTML format and even add HTML tags if you like. It is also a time-saver in that you can create listings for several items that are similar very easily without having to retype everything. Suppose for example, you have ten items that are only slightly different, and you want to use the same description for each one, with only a minor modification. You can just cut and paste the description and make the alterations as needed. Turbo Lister also works with various database and inventory management programs.

- **Seller's Assistant.** The Seller's Assistant comes in two varieties, Pro and Basic. There is a monthly fee involved, although it is quite reasonable. Seller's Assistant gives you several templates that are very easy to use, and all you need to do is insert the details for shipping, tax, and terms. You can also use it to create e-mails to send to your winning bidders. The Pro version adds some extra features, including the ability to schedule your listings, track buyer data, print labels, and automatically submit feedback.

- **Selling Manager.** This is also available in a standard and Pro version. eBay's Selling Manager helps with the management of your listings and in post-sale functions. If you have several items in your inventory, you can use it to manage them and schedule upcoming auctions, track your active listings, and manage all of your post-sale functions including feedback and payments. The Pro version adds some extra useful functions such as generation of profit and loss reports and bulk re-listing of unsold goods. Also in the Pro version, you can download all your sales records in a comma-delimited file format, which you can then upload into a database or spreadsheet program. Another handy feature of Selling Manager is that you can print shipping labels, something you will discover to be quite convenient after hand-writing a few hundred labels.

- **Bulk Catalog Lister.** For high-volume sellers (with at least $5,000 a month in volume), the Bulk Catalog Lister, available for free for qualified sellers, lets you send your inventory into a database, which you can use to create a catalog of listings.

- **Skype.** Most people know about this useful tool recently acquired by eBay. Skype is a Voice over Internet Protocol (VoIP) tool that lets you talk with your customers by voice, over the Internet, without having to worry about long distance charges. You can add either voice or chat communications to your listings to let potential buyers more easily connect with you. You can set your own schedule of availability, and let customers contact you immediately, for quick answers to questions. This is a free service when used on a PC-to-PC basis. Fees are involved when calling from your PC to a regular landline or cellular telephone.

- **Scheduling Function.** You may want to stagger your auctions or set them to begin at a certain time or day or date that you feel is optimal. Fortunately, you do not have to be at your computer at the precise time you want your auction to start. eBay has a built-in scheduler, so you can decide the time and date you want your auction to start. The scheduler can schedule multiple auction listings up to three weeks ahead of time. You may find that auctions do better when they start on a certain day of the week, or you may want to have your auction close at the end of the day instead of earlier to allow people to get home from work and place their final bids before your auction ends. You can schedule all this through the scheduler when you create your auction listing. There are plenty of theories as to when is the best time to end an auction. Many sellers believe that Thursday is the best day to end an auction, although the best way to determine optimal beginning and ending times is just through trial and error. Your customer base is different from other sellers' customer bases, and so the only way to know for sure is just to take time and notice the patterns in your own sales.

- **PayPal Tools.** PayPal has its own set of tools you can take advantage of. The PayPal site's Merchant Tools page is a great place to look, and you will find plenty of useful things there. I know I always like to know the instant money comes in, and the "Instant Payment Notification" feature gives you an interface for real-time purchase confirmation. It sends an immediate notification of any PayPal payments you receive through your Web site. PayPal also has an automated invoicing notice (integrated with eBay, naturally), which will send a PayPal invoice to the buyer immediately after the transaction has been completed.

Third Party Tools

There are dozens of third-party tools available to help you manage your auctions. One such service is Andale, which levies a monthly fee that varies depending on the feature set you choose. Andale includes a one-step auction listing tool and other useful utilities you can use to save time and keep track of your auctions and products. Andale also offers an online database, which you can use to find the average price for different items. This is definitely a useful function when trying to price what you have to sell. Andale includes a counter utility so you can see how many people are visiting your listings. A basic version is available for free, and a pro version is available for a low monthly fee that breaks down the statistics into more detail showing you, for example, traffic per hour and per day.

Another useful third party service you may want to use is image hosting. eBay charges for each picture you upload. The first one is free, and each subsequent one is 15 cents. Frequently, you will want to add three or four pictures of your item at different angles, and if you have hundreds or thousands of auctions going at the same time, your picture hosting fees can add up to a large piece of change. It is often less expensive to host your images through a third party service. Some third party image hosting services, such as Ink Frog, will host your images for a flat fee, and if you have many auctions, this is often significantly cheaper.

Success in eBay also depends on research to determine what is going to sell the best, the best time to start an auction, the best keywords to use, and other statistics. Gathering statistics for your eBay business is important, and you can use a variety of tools, such as Sellathon's ViewTracker, to accomplish this.

ViewTracker gives you an enormous amount of data about each visitor to your auctions, when they visited, what their IP address is, and where they are from. You can even find out the status of your auction at the precise time of each visitor, and whether each visitor is watching your listing. You can also use this tool to determine which search terms your visitors used to find your auctions, and that important piece of information will be very useful in optimizing your search terms for future auctions, since you will know right away what works best.

You will also want to have at least a basic image editor. That digital camera may be able to take good pictures, but you will need to be able to crop the images and sometimes adjust the background or shading to bring out the product better in the photo. While high-end image editors are available and offer a wide range of specialized features, you can get by nicely with a low-cost product. Many digital cameras come with software included, and the free software is usually more than adequate for the basic image editing that you will need to be doing.

The Anonymous Seller

Avoid the temptation to make your online site anonymous. If you are going into business, you have to sacrifice a certain level of privacy. Customers want to know that there is a real person behind the online store, and they want to know who that real person is. Too many potential eBay entrepreneurs decide, "I do not want my name published online!" As a result, they fail very quickly.

Your eBay store is an extension of your own personality and identity, and to be successful you have to share who you are. Create an "About Me" page with a picture of yourself, your brick-and-mortar store if you have one, and legitimate contact information.

Personal Information

When we go into a brick-and-mortar store and see an actual, live person behind the counter, we have a natural tendency to trust that individual. It may not make sense, but we do. We go to the neighborhood drug store or grocery, and there are people there wearing name tags. There is a reason these stores give their employees name tags. If you see that name tag, you will say to yourself, "That's Bob." You will look at Bob's face, and unless he gives you some reason not to trust him, you will naturally give him your trust.

The name tag is used to create an atmosphere of friendliness and trust. Knowing somebody's name and seeing his or her face creates a natural aura of trust for that store. In reality, the person behind that name tag may be the biggest crook you will ever meet, but you do not know that. We still naturally trust somebody with a name tag who is standing behind a counter, and we willingly hand over our credit cards to them.

On the Internet, our natural tendencies are exactly the opposite. Instead of naturally trusting the person behind the counter, or in this case, the "virtual" counter, we naturally distrust them. Despite the fact that e-commerce is growing rapidly, there is still a natural distrust of online commerce and still people who refuse to make electronic transactions on the Internet.

In reality, the Internet is a safer place to spend money than most brick-and-mortar stores, but the perception is the opposite. Although, crime occurs on the Internet, and it is a problem, but there are safeguards in place. Transactions are encrypted. It is very difficult to steal credit card information online. In fact, it is easier for the clerk behind the counter to steal your identity than it is for a cyber thief. Nonetheless, if you run an online business, you have that inherent distrust to overcome. Here is the reason: Nobody can see your face, and nobody knows who you are.

You can overcome that inherent distrust by creating the virtual equivalent of a face and name tag. Here are the very reasons that the vast majority of online stores fail quickly: lack of name recognition and lack of trust.

Creating a cyber store on the Internet may sound like an easy way to make money, but convincing people to shop at your online store is very difficult. If you open up a shop on Main Street, you have the immediate advantage of showing your face and gaining the community's trust; online, they do not know you and cannot see you. Since they have never heard of you before, they will spend their money elsewhere.

The online shops that also have well-established brick-and-mortar presences tend to do the best, and that is simply because they have already created a level of trust with their clientele. People who buy online will be reasonably certain that when they go to **www.Walmart.com**, they are going to receive what they pay for in a reasonable amount of time, it will be what they expect, and nobody is going to steal their money or identity in the process. They believe that because they have seen an actual physical Wal-Mart in their town.

If you do not have the advantage of a physical presence, you have much to overcome. You do have the advantage of being associated with eBay, which has already established a reputation. Whenever an item is listed on eBay, a buyer can click on the "Seller Information" box to see more about the seller's status with eBay and read any feedback that others have left. However, you still are seen as an unknown by the shopper.

You can begin to overcome that by creating a friendly, very personal eBay store. Put your personality into it. Template storefronts are great and easy to create, but tweak them a little bit to include some of yourself there. Put in a picture of yourself standing next to some of your best goods for sale. Make it a personal, friendly picture. If you have kids and a dog, get them to stand next to you for the photo shoot. Use your real name and tell them what your hometown is.

It is quite surprising actually, how many people want to open up an online store, but do not want to tell anybody their real name or hometown. It is understandable to want to protect and isolate yourself from any potential threats that may be out there, but you have to take that risk if you want to be in business. Being in business means being part of a community, and you cannot be part of a community without revealing at least a little bit of who you are.

Of course, you will want to include a well-written "About Me" page, but do not stop there. Include personal details and friendly pictures on every single page. Make your landing page look welcoming and open and include a personal greeting, complete with your name. Make sure there is contact information available. At least include an e-mail address where people can contact you, if nothing else. If you have a brick-and-mortar store, include the address of that store. If you work out of your home, you may not want to show an address, but at least tell people your hometown. Phone numbers are also a good idea, and if possible, put in a separate line just for your business and publish that number.

It is true the e-mail address you publish will be picked up by SPAMbots and you will get unwelcome SPAM e-mail as a result.

You will probably get a few weird phone calls as well, but that is all part of the game.

There are other ways to create that atmosphere of customer trust. Some of it, like the "About Me" page and a few nice pictures, are more about creating a perception of trust. Other techniques are more concrete.

eBay Tips For Success

Throughout this book, I have covered many ways to create eBay success. There are a few things that stand out, however, and the following is a brief list of eBay tips to remember.

1. **Above all else, put yourself and your own personality into your eBay business**. Do not be anonymous. The Internet is inherently anonymous, which can be both an advantage and a disadvantage, but the anonymity is something that will turn away customers. Put yourself into your site, put up a picture of yourself with your family if you have one, and tell people your name. The goal here is to make people think they are buying something from a person not buying something from an Internet Web site.

2. **Avail yourself of the many tools for automation that are available out there.** You do not have to spend a fortune on them, but once your business starts to grow, you will find them to be an absolute necessity. You can only use the pen-and-note card method for so long.

3. **By the same token, do not go overboard.** Too many of those neat little tools can break your budget. Therefore, pace your spending so it tracks with your income. If you are not making enough money yet to buy the fancy $3,000 desktop computer, you probably do not need it and can get by with the one you have for a while longer.

4. **Be careful when writing copy.** Proofread everything, and if you are not competent with the English language, get somebody to help you. A listing full of spelling and grammar mistakes will send customers away quickly. Sure, it is true that the product may still be good, but the impression you are creating when your listing is not well written is that you are not professional, and your customers will not expect you to be professional when you sell them a product either.

5. **Take the opportunity to cross-sell and up-sell whenever possible.** You can often make more money with a customer simply by offering them a companion product.

6. **Avoid the "no minimum" offering.** It is a sure-fire way to lose money on what you are offering. Buyers are pretty sophisticated, and if you do not get any offers until the last minute, you will probably end up having to sell that item for 50 cents and lose money. Even if you have not lost money on the deal, you have not made much, and you have wasted your time. Calculate the minimum amount of money you need to break even and start the bidding around that figure.

7. **Take fulfillment seriously.** The act of taking your product, putting it in a box, and shipping it out can make or break you. The cost of box filling (bubble wrap, Styrofoam) and

the box itself can quickly eat up your entire profit. Buy your bubble wrap in large quantities from large office supply warehouses or wholesalers. If you are sending Priority Mail, use the free boxes from the post office. Minimize your trips to the post office by buying a postal scale/printer and arranging for home pickup.

8. **Do not get too attached to any one product category.** Do not be afraid to try new things. Fads are fads. Take them for what they are. Make money from your product category while it lasts and then move on.

9. **eBay has many product listing variations, each of which adds to the cost of your listing.** Use them sparingly. You do not have to add all of the extra boldface listings and front-page features to everything you have for sale. Save all the extras for the high dollar items that will generate the most competition, and use the basic listing format for your routine, every-day items.

10. **Your eBay business is a business, not a hobby, so treat it like one.** Give it the priority it deserves, quit your day job when it becomes appropriate to do so, and put all the time, effort, and resources into your eBay business you need to make it successful.

Robert Sachs, RKS Solutions

Listen: Spend time each week reading through the various eBay discussion boards. Tapping into that pool of knowledge can be daunting. There are folks in there who have been selling successfully for years, and they are generally willing to share with anyone who asks. But please READ before you POST. There are some questions that have been asked so many times that it's very easy to find the answers you are looking for without having to ask those same questions yet again.

Research: Before you buy that gross of widgets, do some research and find out if there really IS a market for them, or if that's just a line the seller is using to move their product. Learn to use the research tools available, free or by subscription, and spend the time needed to determine if that great new thing really is.

Make the time to stop and smell the roses. eBay is not the meaning of life. It is an opportunity to do something else, something different, something fun. It is not the reason for your existence, and it will still be there tomorrow, even if you take this afternoon off. Balance is the key to success. You need time to unwind and relax.

About the Author

Dan Blacharski

Dedication

"To my beautiful wife Be, you are my inspiration."

Dan Blacharski has been a professional writer and online entrepreneur for over 15 years, and is a graduate of the University of California, Santa Cruz. He has written eight books and ghost-written several others; has produced thousands of print and online features, articles, and columns; and has helped many Internet companies jump into the fray. A refugee from Silicon Valley, Dan was there during the "dotcom boom," witnessing first-hand the incredible rise and fall of countless empires, and gaining insight into what makes a new-era Internet company succeed or fail. He worked directly with many of these companies, helping them to refine their messaging. Currently, he is also a contributing analyst for Compass Intelligence, a virtual "think tank" that provides world-class market analytic research.

Dan is listed in Marquis' Who's Who, and as a long-time industry observer and visionary, has often been at the forefront of new innovations in the area of Internet commerce, chronicling their creation, working with start-ups to make them happen, and getting an inside look into where those innovations will lead us in the future.

One of Dan's own entrepreneurial dotcom ventures is We Know The Answers **http://www.weknowtheanswers.com**, an advertiser-supported online informational site. He currently lives in South Bend, Indiana with his lovely wife Charoenkwan, where they enjoy spending time renovating their 120-year-old Victorian home; but having never gotten quite used to the frigid Midwest, they spend their winters in Bangkok.

eBay Terminology

A

ABSENTEE BID A bid placed by users before the start of the auction.

ADMINISTRATIVE CANCELLATION When the eBay administration cancels a bid or auction.

ANNOUNCEMENT BOARDS Similar to a message board, the eBay announcement boards provide information on updates and current events.

ASKING PRICE The price asked by the seller.

AUCTION CURRENCY The type of currency for a specific auction decided by the seller.

AUCTION-STYLE LISTING Placing an item for sale and selling it to the highest bidder.

B

BID CANCELLATION A buyer or seller may cancel a bid.

BID INCREMENT The amount a bid is raised.

BID RETRACTION Cancellation of a bid.

BIDDER REGISTRATION REQUIREMENTS The requirements that must be met before a user is allowed to bid.

BIDDER SEARCH A search for the items that a member has placed bids on.

BIDDING To place a bid on an item.

BLOCK BIDDERS A way to prevent users from bidding on your items.

BUY IT NOW A listing that allows a buyer to purchase an item for the seller's set price without waiting for the auction to end.

BUYER'S PREMIUM Amount a buyer pays an auction house for all purchases in a live auction.

C

CATEGORY LISTING A category that an item goes under when listed for organization.

CHANGED USER ID ICON An icon that notifies viewers that a member has changed his user ID in the past 30 days.

COMPLETED LISTING SEARCH Search for items that have ended within the last 15 days.

CYBERCRIME A technology crime related to a computer and the Internet.

D

DISPUTE CONSOLE The area on eBay where buyers and sellers dispute problems related to their auction.

DUTCH AUCTION A listing with many similar items for sale.

E

eBay An auction service on the Web.

eBay SHOP A shop that sells eBay collectibles.

eBay STORE A Web site that offers all items being sold by an individual seller.

eBay TIME The official eBay Time correlated with the time of day in San Jose, California.

eBay TOOLBAR A toolbar that can be downloaded and used in your Web browser.

E-MAIL Electronic mail.

EXPERT CONTACT Usually the seller, the expert contact provides all the information on upcoming auctions.

F

FAIR WARNING A warning from the seller that the auction will be closed.

FEATURED LISTING A marketing service where sellers can have their item placed at the top of the listing page in the "Featured" section.

FEEDBACK A rating a buyer and seller receive after a transaction is completed.

FEEDBACK SCORE The number of feedbacks the seller or buyer has received.

FEEDBACK STAR A star on a particular seller's listing that varies by color with the amount of feedback the seller has received.

FINAL VALUE The final value that a listing sells for.

FINAL VALUE FEE A fee charged by eBay at the end of the auction.

FIXED PRICE FORMAT A format mostly used for "Buy It Now" listings where the price is unchanging.

FLAME An angry feedback.

G

GENTLY USED Description of an item that has been used but does not show wear.

GIFT SERVICE A service offered by a seller that allows the buyer to purchase gift wrapping and shipment directly to the recipient.

H

HOT ITEM An item that has received more than 30 bids.

I

ID VERIFIED Shows other users that a seller has a confirmed identity.

INDEFINITE SUSPENSION Suspension of a user with no reinstatement date.

INSERTION FEE A fee to sell an item.

INTERNET MERCHANT ACCOUNT An account where a seller can accept credit cards online.

ITEM LOOKUP A way of searching for an item by item number.

L

LIVE AUCTIONS Real time auctions online.

LOT A group of similar items for auction "by the lot."

M

MARKUP The price that an item is increased to reach retail price.

MAXIMUM BID The maximum amount a buyer will pay for an item.

MEMBER PROFILE A site that informs buyers about the seller's feedback and customer comments.

MERGE Combining several eBay user IDs.

MERGE ACCOUNTS To combine more than one eBay account.

MINIMUM BID The lowest price that can be used to bid on an item.

MY eBay The place on eBay where the user controls all aspects of their eBay business.

N

NEW LISTING ICON Indication that an item has been placed within the last 24 hours.

NEW MEMBER ICON An icon that represents a member who has been registered less than 30 days.

O

OPENING VALUE Starting price.

OUTBID To make a higher bid (than another bidder).

P

PASSWORD A word or group of words and numbers used to verify the user.

PAYMENT GATEWAY Program used to process and authorize payments.

PAYPAL A free account used to pay for items online.

BUYER PROTECTION A protection worth up to $1,000 for buyers who pay with PayPal.

PICTURE ICON Tells buyers that the listing includes a picture of the item.

PIRACY Illegally copying copyrighted material.

POWERSELLER A user who has a 98 percent positive feedback and a high volume of items listed.

PRIVATE AUCTION LISTING A listing where the bidder's User IDs are hidden.

PROCESSOR A credit card processor.

PROXY BIDDING A form of bidding where a user enters his maximum bid and eBay automatically bids when another user places his bid.

R

REGISTERED USER A user who is registered with eBay by providing contact information.

RE-LISTING To resell an item if it did not sell on the first auction.

RESERVE PRICE A secret price that the seller must receive to sell the item.

S

SECOND CHANCE OFFER An offer to the second highest bidder when the winning bidder fails to pay.

SECURE SERVER A secure server used to process credit card information.

SELL SIMILAR ITEM A feature that allows sellers to sell a similar item without inputting all the previous information.

SELLER SEARCH To search for a seller.

SELLER'S ASSISTANT A selling tool that helps with buying, listing, and selling on eBay.

SELLER'S RETURN POLICY The return policy stated by the seller on their listing.

SHILL BIDDING Placing bids artificially to raise the price of an auction.

STARTING PRICE The price at which the seller opens the auction

STORE INVENTORY FORMAT A way to list an item at a set price from the user's store.

T

TITLE SEARCH A search method of looking for an item by entering a keyword.

TURBO LISTING A program that is designed to allow users to create listings for auctions quickly and easily.

U

UNPAID ITEM PROCESS A process used when the seller does not receive payment for an item.

USER AGREEMENT Terms and conditions eBay users accept before they become a member.

USER ID eBay user name that a buyer or seller operates under.

V

VENDOR A supplier.

VERIFIED USER A user that has verified contact information.

VIEWING Watching the auction in real time while online or offline.

W

WANT IT NOW An area of eBay where the buyer posts and item he wants, and the seller contacts him if she has them.

INDEX

References

Shipping Resources

DHL	www.dhl.com
eBay	http://pages.ebay.com/services/buyandsell/shippingcenter9.html
	http://pages.ebay.com/services/buyandsell/shippinginternational.html
Express Mail	www.usps.com/shipping/expressmail.htm
FedEx	FedEx.com
Greyhound Express	www.shipgreyhound.com
Media Mail	www.usps.com/businessmail101/classes/packageServices.htm
Priority Mail	www.usps.com/businessmail101/classes/priority.htm
Stamps.com	www.stamps.com
Selling Manager Pro	http://pages.ebay.com/help/sell/printing-invoice.html#bulk_printing
Uline	www.uline.com
UPS	UPS.com
U.S. Postal Service	U.S. Postal Service.com

Listing Software

AAA Seller	www.aaaseller.com
All My Auctions for Sellers	www.rajeware.com/auction/index.html
Alysta AuctionMaker Standard	www.alysta.com/software/auctionmaker.htm Andale www.andale.com/corp/products/products.jsp
Auction Hawk	www.auctionhawk.com
Auction Wizard 2000	www.auctionwizard2000.com

AuctionGenie	www.luxcentral.com/auctiongenie
AuctionHelper	www.auctionhelper.com/ah/main/main.asp
AuctionSage	www.auctionsagesoftware.com
AuctionSound	www.auctionsound.com
AuctionTamer	www.auctiontamer.com/atindex.htm
AuctionTeller	www.auctionteller.com
AuctionWagon Store Manager G2	www.auctionwagon.com
Auctiva Power Tools	http://classic.auctiva.com/products/Download.aspx
AuktionMaster.NET	www.pages.auctionWeb.info
bidmachine	www.bidmachine.com
Blackthorne	www.pages.ebay.com/blackthorne
CARad	www.carad.com
ChannelAdvisor Merchant	www.channeladvisor.com/solutions/merch_overview.asp
ChannelAdvisor Pro	www.pro.channeladvisor.com/pro/default.asp
Consignment Companion	www.auctionadvantage.biz/Products/Consignment%20Companion.htm
CORESense for eBay	www.coresense.com/products/sbebay/index.html
DEK AuctionManager	www.dekauctionmanager.com
Easy AuctionTools	www.auctiontools.net
eSellerPro	www.esellerpro.com
Estates-On-Line.com	www.estates-on-line.com
ezebase	www.ezebase.com/products/index.htm
Hungry Gopher	www.hungrygopher.com
Infopia Marketplace Manager	www.infopia.com/products/mm.shtml
inkFrog	www.inkfrog.com
kAuction	www.kinem.com
Kyozou	www.kyozou.com
Liberty TA Resaleworld	www.resaleworld.com/L4TA.php
MarketBlast	www.marketblast.com
MarketPlacePro	www.marketplacepro.com
Marketworks	www.marketworks.com
Meridian	www.noblespirit.com
Mpire Launcher & Builder	www.mpire.com/products/launcher.html
My Auction	www.database-central.com/myauction/index.html
Picture Manager	www.pages.ebay.com/picture_manager
Seller Sourcebook	www.sellersourcebook.com
Seller's Assistant	www.pages.ebay.com/sellers_assistant
Selling Manager	www.pages.ebay.com/selling_manager pro

SendPal	www.sendpal.com/public/service.aspx
ShipWorks	www.interapptive.com
Shooting Star	www.foodogsoftware.com
SpareDollar	www.sparedollar.com/corp
SpoonFeeder	www.spoonfeeder.com
Trak Auctions	www.jwcinc.net/Info/AuctionManagement.aspx
Turbo Lister	www.pages.ebay.com/turbo_lister/download.html
Turbo Lister 2	www.pages.ebay.com/turbo_lister/
Vendi	www.vendisoftware.com
Vendio Sales Manager	wsacp.vendio.com/my/acp/promo_choose.html
You Can Bill Me	www.youcanbillme.com
zdrop	www.ztradingindustries.com/products/zdrop.aspx
Zoovy	www.zoovy.com

Search Engines

AllTheWeb	www.alltheWeb.com
AltaVista	www.altavista.com
AOL Search	http://search.aol.com/aolcom/Webhome
Ask Jeeves	www.askjeeves.com
Google	www.google.com
HotBot	www.hotbot.com
LookSmart	www.looksmart.com
Lycos	www.lycos.com
MSN Search	www.msnsearch.com
Netscape Search	http://channels.netscape.com/search
Open Directory	http://dmoz.org
Yahoo	www.yahoo.com

eBay Resources

"About Me" Guidelines	http://pages.ebay.comhelp/policies/listing-aboutme.html
"About Me" Page	http://pages.ebay.com/help/account/about-me.html
Become an Education Specialist	http://www.poweru.net/ebay/index.asp
Best Offers	http://pages.ebay.com/help/sell/best-offer.html
"buy it now"	http://pages.ebay.com/help/sell/bin.html
Cross-promotions	http://pages.ebay.com/help/sell/cp-overview.html
eBay Keywords	http://pages.ebay.com/keywords/
eBay Live!	http://pages.ebay.com/ebaylive/
eBay Motors	www.motors.ebay.com
eBay Pulse	http://pulse.ebay.com/

eBay Store Promotions	http://pages.ebay.com/help/specialtysites/promoting-your-store.html
eBay University	http://pages.ebay.com/university/index.html
Final Value Fees (FVF)	www.pages.ebay.com/help/sell/fvf.html
Fixed Price	http://pages.ebay.com/help/sell/fixed_price.html
Half.com	www.half.com
Marketplace Research	http://pages.ebay.com/marketplace%5Fresearch/
PowerSeller	http://pages.ebay.com/services/buyandsell/welcome.html
PowerU Education Specialist Directory	http://www.poweru.net/ebay/student/searchIndex.asp
PS Criteria	http://pages.ebay.com/services/buyandsell/powerseller/criteria.html
TA Directory	http://tradingassistant.ebay.com/ws/eBayISAPI.dll?TradingAssistant&page=main
Trading Assistants	http://pages.ebay.com/tradingassistants/hire-trading-assistant.html
Unpaid Item Process	http://pages.ebay.com help/tp/unpaid-item-process.html

Other Online Resources

PayPal	www.paypal.com
iOffer	www.ioffer.com
Babel Fish Translator	www.babelfish.altavista.com
Google Adwords	http://services.google.com/marketing/links/ US-HA-CMBNINE2/
sharptradingcompany	www.stores.ebay.com/Sharp-Trading-Company
silvercreekconsignment	www.stores.ebay.com/SilverCreekConsignment
stephintexas	www.stores.ebay.com/TEXAS-STATE-OF-MIND
sunnking	www.stores.ebay.com/Sunnking
thebetterbaglady	www.stores.ebay.com/Tongue-In-Chic
thebiglittlestore	www.stores.ebay.com/the-big-little-store
themesnthings1	www.stores.ebay.com/THEMES-N-THINGS
Webauctionexpert	www.Webauctionexperts.com
with-a-twist	www.stores.ebay.com/The-Endless-Emporium
xena-angel	www.stores.ebay.com/Angels-Closet-and-Gifts
yardleyplace	www.auctionworkspr.com

Recommended Reading

How and Where to Locate the Merchandise to Sell on eBay: Insider Information You Need to Know from the Experts Who Do It Every Day

More than 724,000 Americans report that eBay is their source of income. Finding customers is not a problem—locating quality items to sell is the challenge. Learn where to find products that you can buy for a few cents on the dollar and resell for massive profits! You will be provided detailed information on: wholesalers, drop shippers, closeouts, discontinued merchandise, overstocks, customer returns, liquidators, close out firms, foreign and domestic manufacturers, places to look in your area, and more. You will learn to become a product sourcing pro and make money on eBay! All types of products are covered.

ISBN-10: 0-910627-87-8 • ISBN-13: 978-0-910627-87-0

288 Pgs • Item #HWL-01 • $24.95

The eBay Success Chronicles: Secrets and Techniques eBay PowerSellers Use Every Day to Make Millions by Angela C. Adams

"An important part of success on eBay is learning to cross market merchandise between stores and auctions and to find a niche and brand your name. This assures return customers, which is what every business thrives on. Angela's book is a serious lesson on how to do both. From cover to cover it teaches you success on eBay from those who are successful. Highly recommended for anyone who hopes to have a business on eBay—part-time or full-time." —Joyce Banbury, eBay Certified Education Specialist

ISBN-10: 0-910627-64-9 • ISBN-13: 978-0-910627-64-1

408 Pgs • Item #ESC-02 • $21.95

The Ultimate Guide to Search Engine Marketing: Pay Per Click Advertising Secrets Revealed by Bruce C. Brown

You can increase your Web site traffic by more than 1,000 percent through Pa Per Click advertising (PPC). Successful PPC advertising ensures that your text ads reach the right audience while your business only pays for the clicks you receive! Learn the secrets of executing a successful, cost-effective campaign. Learn the six steps to a successful campaign: Keyword Research, Copy Editing, Setup and Implementation, Bid Management, Performance Analysis, Return on Investment, and Reporting and Avoiding PPC Fraud.

ISBN-10: 0-910627-99-1 • ISBN-13: 978-0-910627-99-3

288 Pgs • Item #UGS-01 • $24.95

How to Use the Internet to Advertise, Promote and Market Your Business or Web Site – With Little or No Money by Bruce C. Brown

"With so many how-to-build-your-own-Web-business books on the market, this book exceeds all with up-to-date information, legitimate, low-cost, and effective Internet marketing strategies." — Jennifer Somogyi, Founder, The Professional Women's Outreach Organization

ISBN-10: 0-910627-57-6 • ISBN-13: 978-0-910627-57-3

288 Pgs • Item #HIA-01 • $24.95